Songs of My Life & Death

Songs of
My Life
& Death

The Poetry of
Peter Hartley

Grosvenor House
Publishing Limited

This book is published by
Grosvenor House Publishing Ltd
Link House
140 The Broadway, Tolworth, Surrey, KT6 7HT.
www.grosvenorhousepublishing.co.uk

A CIP record for this book
is available from the British Library

Paperback ISBN 978-1-80381-329-5
Hardback ISBN 978-1-80381-061-4

To Dina

No need to ask where will it end: we know.
This creeping palsy no-one can reverse,
The news each day by day is ever worse
Than yesterday's. If only we could glow
With childhood's bloom forever and forgo
Our troubles on this earth, nor need rehearse
Each day as if it were our last. Averse
To tears, self-pity she will never show,

Nor share the fears I feel for her. The night
Is painless, though she looks so worn and drawn,
And through the veil of dark some inner sight
Reveals a sky now silvered with the dawn.
As far horizons near, let hers shine bright,
And brighter still the gleaming of the light.

To Dina

In Memoriam

"Thank you for letting me come home," she said
To me the night she died and I, tongue-tied,
I could not speak though heaven knows I tried.
"I fear the night," she said to me, "I dread
The coming dawn. No longer shall we tread
Barefoot on turf, no longer step outside
To hear the blackbird's song at eventide,
Nor dwell as one to happy silence wed."

Your loving spirit earthbound heretofore,
By angels flown aloft and fleet and far,
I'll find you, follow you forevermore
While folded in the arms of Christ you are.
When you came home with me that fateful night
It wasn't me you saw turn off the light.

Contents

Front cover photographs

Top row (L-R)
Beside the Boudhanath Stupa, Kathmandu
Climbing the Chudleigh Overhang
The Great Wall of China at Badaling
Street scene in Marrakech, Morocco

Middle row
Pinnewala Elephant Orphanage, Sri Lanka
Empire State Building, New York
The Old Man of Hoy, Orkney
Machu Picchu, Peru
Everest, 8848m, from the air

Bottom row
Commercial Street, Lerwick, Shetland
The Taj Mahal, Agra, India
A Mosque in Uzbekistan
Fingal's Cave, Staffa, Inner Hebrides

Back cover photographs

Top row
The top of Mont Blanc, 4808m, its shadow cast on the clouds.
At the summit cross of the Dom, 4545m
View from Monte Rosa, 4634m
At the summit cornice of Obergabelhorn, 4063m, storm brewing

Middle row
On top of the Matterhorn, 4478m
Busy market near Aguas Calientes, Peru
Miniature painting of Vida, by the author's mother
Suq Street, Luxor, Egypt
New Zealand's Ngauruhoe, 2291m, and Mount Ruapehu, 2797m

Bottom row
Barney, cocker spaniel, on North Uist, Outer Hebrides
Footprints on Weisshorn, 4505m
Climbers on summit of Dent Blanche, 4357m
Gentoo penguins at Port Lockroy, Antarctica

Foreword

Omitting only a few atrocious verses that were published in his school magazine some fifty years ago, this volume contains nearly every poem the author has ever written. All were composed over the space of three years but they represent many of the joys and some of the sorrows of a lifetime.

They touch upon several of the author's past and current interests: his mountaineering days in the European Alps and elsewhere; rock-climbing, mainly in Devon and Cornwall, as a student; a fascination for certain periods of English history with intermittent spells of researching his own; cryptic crosswords; Gerard Manley Hopkins; Thomas Hardy; baroque music, especially the oratorios of Handel; and, before everything seized up, long-distance fell-walking. The earth's polar regions have held a long-standing appeal for him, fostered by two trips to Antarctica and holidays visiting Spitsbergen and Norway's far north, while an interest in travel in general has led to his visiting over sixty countries around the world. But the UK is also represented here with poems on the Western Isles, among his favourite places on earth were it not for the rain and the infernal midges.

These poems also introduce one or two of the author's more contentious views, as for example what he sees, from the standpoint of a former paintings restorer, as the steady decline in technical competence in fine art; and the question of whether or not animals have souls. There are poems here describing the bustling self-importance of the penguin, the self-serving intractability of the cat, and several (an unhealthy number, some might say) about the irrepressible bonhomie of the Labrador retriever. He makes no apology for this, believing them to be among the most benign creatures on earth and some of the easiest to get on with.

During the writing of this volume's predecessor the author's beloved Dina was struck down by motor neurone disease, a particularly cruel illness for which there is no cure and one whose prognosis is terminal. In nearly sixty poems that speak of Dina, including the two dedicatory sonnets, not one word is rhetorical: her fortitude and stoicism during this, her greatest trial, were as inspiring as they were exemplary.

Prompted by her illness and death much of the poetry in this book is permeated with the darkness of suffering humanity, with physical pain and mental anguish, the infinite pathos in the deaths of innocent and helpless animals, bereavement, unrequited love, the blackness of hell, Gallipoli and the apocalypse. Repeatedly these poems speak of grief and the focus of that grief. The focus is Dina and the grief is my own. It wasn't planned like that from the outset but that is the direction in which it has developed over the past several months and that is where the poetry has ineluctably led me. Moving from the third person singular pronoun to the first at this point makes me feel as though I have crossed a frontier of confidentiality, stepping away for a moment from a grief that is universal experience to one that is private and suffered alone. Bridging the two for me gives this book some justification, for there is surely much comfort and reassurance in the knowledge that although we may suffer our bereavement alone there is somebody in the next room grieving too.

Grief sometimes brings catharsis but sometimes also it oversteps the mark to self-indulgence. It can be difficult to know where one ends and the other begins, but wherever the border lies it is true that I did not always treat Dina as well as I might have done, and certainly not as well as she deserved.

In writing these poems, I must say, I had no intention of singing her praises or becoming her hagiographer. But is it not true that the more humble the life the more gratified we are when we find it to have been a charitable one? It is the Cure d'Ars and Mary Magdalen we admire before some of those ancient and mediaeval popes with all their pomp and panoply, whose office seems to have conferred free passage to sainthood.

Dina's life was free from pretence and affectation, full of openness and honesty and the empathy that Thomas Hardy advocated as loving kindness. It can do no harm to extol a virtuous life.

Too late I found admirable qualities in Dina that I scarcely noticed, or only partly acknowledged to myself, or to her, while she lived. Runner-up on the list of these qualities in the fifteen years I knew her was her selflessness, but the greatest of all was her formidable courage in adversity, in physical pain and in mental anguish, and this was of course most apparent only towards the end when she was dying. Too late I recognised faults in me that might have been amended by her example. Always too late, always too late.

But it wasn't too late for the Good Thief on Calvary and surely the very existence of right and wrong in humankind gives us reason for being and postulates the existence of an after-life, beginning, for many of us, with some halfway house wherein we might rectify our mistakes if so inclined, make recompense for our wrongs, acknowledge our faults and the virtues of others; a place for settling old scores amicably and for Any Other Business. We'll call it Purgatory.

This book could never have been solely about grief. There are memories I would not exchange for the world, that I could not forget if I would. Very few of us, I imagine, can sustain anguish and remorse for every second of every day. Grief doesn't work like that. Some kindly dispensation of nature will always lull us from time to time into a Lethean state of abstraction that allows us to contemplate and relive the most vivid and joyful experiences from our past, from our daydreams and the products of our imagination with genuine happiness unadulterated by wistfulness and regrets. These poems, some of them, are welcome reminders for me of occasional periods of uncomplicated happiness in youth, when the certainties of death and bereavement seemed light-years away.

There are poems here about some of the remoter far-flung island groups of Scotland, including St Kilda, which I first saw fifty years ago from the tip of the half-submerged wedge of Eaval, forty-odd miles to the east. Islands like these have always fascinated me through the hardihood and resourcefulness of those who once wrested a living from them, and all have their own stories to tell.

There are poems about the seasons, four about mountaineers and five about a single painting by Salvador Dali. And Jimi Hendrix seems to have made it here somehow by virtue of his having lived next door to Handel two-and-a-half centuries too late for a showdown over which of the two was the greater musician. At one time it might have been a simple choice to judge the respective merits of Dufy and Duccio perhaps, or Raphael and Rothko; in music Chopin and Cage. But the outcome of a vote between any of these pairs might not be quite so conclusive today where we find Emin is better known than van Eyck.

Peter Hartley,
Manchester, 2023

Part One

Of Labradors & Penguins

1 Art
&
Music

Michelangelo's David

No-one can ever see the man behind
These opaque eyes that never shed his tears,
Or feel the fears that simmered in his mind.
No longer does he hear the jeers and cheers
For that unequal combat with the foe.
He sees nothing, nor could he. Through those eyes
Of stone not even Michelangelo
Could let us see his own Italic skies.

There's something enigmatic we perceive
In statuary, shorn of intellect,
Tongue-tied, unable to explain, conceive,
Convey their thoughts to us, or interject
If we are wrong. Free-standing some may be,
All standing free, remote from you and me.

A Fire Extinguisher

Though technical accomplishment held sway
For centuries, some artists of today
Will doubtless scorn such talent as passé.
Once art stood on its merits and would say
"My worth resides in what you see in me,
Not what your facile pseudo-intellect
Extrapolates from what you *think* you see,
Confected with the guff we all expect."

Collectors, artists, critics must have all
Conspired in symbiosis to inspire
Tate Modern's latest coup: upon the wall
Its finest purchase yet, a smart new fire
Extinguisher. Just think of all that hype
It garnered, hanging there among the tripe.

A Picture of a Horse

While at a gallery one day appears
A little mob of children, come to see
Some Pollock drips, a few of Rothko's smears,
And several of Picasso's ears set free
To roam about the same side of his face.
Their teacher showed a painting of a horse.
"And that's supposed to be a horse, in case
You can't read what the label says of course,"

She said, and then a little boy piped "So
Why isn't it a horse?" and she was at
A loss. It looked more like a portmanteau,
A set of bagpipes or a stovepipe hat,
But gave one the *impression* of a horse.
Why wasn't it a picture of a horse?

The Mouth Organ

A bel esprit, a skilful maestro too,
A philharmonic connoisseur he plays
The mouth organ. A virtuoso who
Tops Paganini in so many ways.
He segues from his rallentandos to
Abrupt accelerandos with such verve
And such panache: give credit where it's due,
It's well deserved, he's such a flawless oeuvre.

And that harmonica's so resonant,
A full symphony orchestra's trombones
Could never make a sound more consonant
Despite its diatonic semitones.
But what a noise! While one may be a curse
The sound of two is something rather worse.

Poetry Today

If elevated thought had ever been
The least criterion of excellence
In poetry, why should it then be seen
Today as simply of no consequence?
If rhyme was good enough in Shakespeare's time
And rhythm beats in Keats and Chaucer, Blake
And Dryden why then, why is rhyme a crime
And rhythm a mistake for heaven's sake?

Free verse, a curse at worst, its mastery
A hash of slapdash balderdash and bull,
Such tripe the tritest poetastery
Disposed in random rows is just as dull.
Who knows why those to metric rhyme averse
Compose such awful prose and call it verse.

The Dark Ages

What cultural wasteland could have produced
The Book of Durrow and the Book of Kells?
A barren tasteless age it introduced
The Gothic with the greatest church in Wells.
And dark their ages were but for their part
They'd not the consummate effrontery
To call a pile of bricks a work of art,
To pickle sharks, make the discovery

That hype and bluster and a name that sells
Can turn the most outrageous bottled fart
Into the most dramatic work of art.
The Book of Durrow and the Book of Kells:
Those humble scribes, their fame no-one proclaims:
How *could* we, for they didn't leave their names.

Millais's "Winter Fuel"

In eighteen seventy-three an autumn glim.
Here sitting on a barrow-tram a lass,
A mickle of dead leaves on each sawn limb,
A brushwood rickle skailed upon the grass.

Beneath a wreath of tangled twigs the dray,
With knotty snarls of timber piled on high,
Stands dreary on a sodden bridleway,
Above it nothing but a sodden sky.

And parchment-like the birch-bark, paper-thin,
The weighty oak more steeve and stronger too,
They've dwined long sin', bog asphodel and whin,
There's nothing to relieve the dowie hue.

And on the moss the muirburn sears the earth
Beyond the drystane dykes and on the brae,
The smoke in smudges scudding south to Perth,
Is carried with the winter wind away.

The wind! We cannot hear those vicious squalls
From paint on canvas, though they crack the boughs
Of mighty oak trees in the draughty halls
Of Boreas, and rouse the cows that browse

The lea-rig stubble, for the want of grass,
To huddle in the mud. We cannot feel
The wind through walls, but join the highland lass
Outside for what the mind's eye might reveal.

And stepping into Millais's picture, how
The wind blows cold among the trees, and moans
And soughs daylong around each naked bough,
It coils through ancient Birnam Wood and groans.

And here she sits, nor troubled, so says she,
Nor saddened by the falling of the leaves.
She spares no cares for frail mortality,
She'll wait till she grows old before she grieves.

Ahead her years stretch soundlessly and so
They'll meet the silence of all ages past,
Eternity as boundless as we know
The skies and seas illimitably vast.

Eternity, that certainty wherefore
This trial tenure of our mortal phase,
As distant as the summit of Drum Mor,
Infinity the limits of her gaze.

But she's long gone from us, though on each ben
The profiles that she knew remain the same.
Today we see them as she saw them then,
As one lies captured still inside this frame.

A man who viewed it, at the time unfamed,
Was G M Hopkins, so renowned today,
And in his journal he for one proclaimed
There's little in the painting to convey

The sorrow of the fall. Death and decay
Are seldom though so very far away
As stoat from rabbit's throat, as pope a prey
To osprey, pygmy shrew may be to jay,

The vole transfixed by stabbing heronshaw;
From March the carnage as the crofter damns
The hoodie crow that struts about the moor
And plucks the een from helpless living lambs.

Why *should* she weep to hear the final purl
of music from the wretched starving merle,
If from his palette Millais can portray
In falling leaves the promise of the May?

In crisp harsh light the pallid autumn fields
Provide no bield before the evening glow.
Long shadows stretch out over yearly yields,
In stook and stack, in sheaf and threave they go.

But in this tableau she looks out of place,
An afterthought, and seemingly beside
The point, redundant to the scene, her face
Averted and her waeful gaze outside

The confines of the picture space; she'll weep
Now, dread the weary winter of her span,
She'll cry to mark the passing fall, in deep
Despair, she knows not how long hoping can

Stave off the gloom, while she in tender years
May pine without the wisdom of her eld,
She'll keep her level standing with her peers
Their foolish lives her foolish life impelled.

Our journey to adulthood we forget,
Too painful to recall and full of woe,
Yet over worthless goals we'll cease to fret,
Forgo self-loathing, narcissism, so

Too every other defect of the young.
It's very hard to see how, to a lass
Who's sitting on a barrow-tram among
The leaves, a facial blemish or a mass

Of dull camstairy hair, or awkward gait,
Outweighs the import of a stour between
Great nations, plague or famine, flood or state
Of war when we are barely seventeen.

In questing what her future years may bring,
Her only hope may lie in her decease,
While every new renaissance of the spring
Inexorably leads to her release.

The pains of adolescence, from the wrong
Word spoken to the wrong time chosen for
Our clumsy gaffes, our scrawny limbs too long
To cope with gaucheries we all deplore,

To abject terrors and to panic prone,
In company moods plummet like a stone:
It's safer if you're sitting on your own,
It's so much safer being all alone.

But in that moment frozen in slow time
She cannot know how nearly she is grown:
Imago, set to spread her wings and climb
From earth to sky, her element. Her own.

Her time is right, as beautiful a sight
As monarch, cardinal or admiral,
As comma, copper, argus and as bright,
But like the mayfly as ephemeral.

In eighteen seventy-three an autumn glim,
She sat upon a barrow-tram. Alas!
Long dead with every sawn and broken limb,
And brushwood rickle skailed upon the grass.

Scots Words in The Chambers Dictionary

Glim; glimpse. *Mickle;* a great quantity. *Rickle;* a loose heap.
Skailed; scattered. *Steeve;* sturdy. *Dwined;* wasted away. *Sin';*
since. *Dowie;* dull, dismal. *Muirburn;* seasonal burning of
heather. *Lea-rig;* unploughed grass field. *Drum;* ridge.
Drystane dykes; drystone walls. *Brae;* hill slope. *Ben;* mountain
peak. *Een;* eyes. *Merle;* blackbird. *Bield;* protection. *Waeful;*
pitiful. *Camstairy;* unruly, quarrelsome. *Stour;* battle.

Handel's Messiah: A Prayer

With "Soli Deo Gloria," as found
Initialled on his score, does he restate
His pious self-effacement and relate
How zealous work will see His glory crowned.
Cathedral stalls and concert halls redound
To His acclaim, as Saul and Samson rate
With Solomon among the very great
To let an even greater work resound.

For God's amanuensis was he sent,
This instrument of The Omnipotent.
His timpani, strings, hautboys and keyboard,
With clarions bright and solo voices scored,
His chorus praise Him in memoriam,
And Ad Majorem Dei Gloriam.

Three Muses or Nine

While Clio's satisfied herstory's true
Should Calliope's epic verse conspire
With Melpomene's tragic point of view,
Euterpe's chirpy flute, Erato's lyre
Embellish Thalia's comedic flights?
Their music with Terpsichore's ballet
Transport Urania to cosmic heights,
To sacred Polyhymnia convey?

But some admit just three, so to confuse
Your muse, bemuse her with the latest news:
Our cognoscenti are novenary
Though supernumerary some may be.
While numbers of these literati vary
At female rhyme their skills are legendary.

Musical Profundity

A Handel oratorio can sing
Within as Palestrina's masses may;
As Schubert's lieder, Bach's cantatas bring
For us their brightest harmonies today.
Compare these to the trite words and the pout
And posture of an adolescent band
Of would-be slebs and wannabees about
To drown each other out; or that unplanned

Keyboard concerto that could well no doubt
Produce the same discordant chords of sorts,
Some strings at random hampered by a trout;
Or coughs and sniffs and incidental snorts
In four-and-a-half minutes of background
Sound. Is this *music,* be it so profound?

The Beauty of Concrete

Hawksmoor and Wren did so much more
For us than rebuild after the Great Fire,
And they would blench to see what none admire
Today, the faceless flats we all abhor,
Spread far and wide,
those blank walls more and more
Conspire to bring us down, or to inspire
Graffiti, that seem almost to require
The drabness of post-war architecture.

The sort of cityscape the soul desires,
Picks Pugin's gothic churches, all replete
With pinnacles and crockets, soaring spires.
Engulfed by tons of reinforced concrete,
The only use for this, the only place
For it, to ruin every living space.

The Arnolfini Portrait

For some van Eyck might warrant scant acclaim
Today, laboriously painting what he made
Us see in outline, colour, light and shade;
Whose tableaux frozen on oak panels frame
The most minutely detailed scenes and claim
Enraptured awe. In mastery displayed
Six hundred years ago his brush conveyed
What he saw now, for still we see the same.

Should Emin view his art might she dismiss
It all as lesser work than hers because
She's better known than van Eyck ever was?
And can she see the oddity in this?
Perhaps her confidence in private sinks.
We're left to wonder what she really thinks.

The Hebrides Overture

What Mendelssohn out of his head can wring
From nature's chords, what crashing seas of sound!
With growling shag and rock-dove's clopping wing,
The oystercatcher's piping din. Thus bound
Transfixed did Ulysses hear sirens sing.
As Fingal's Cave responds to laughing gull
So vast cathedral walls with echoes ring
To fill the vaulted cavern of his skull.

Can any artist's medium acquaint
Us with those wild tempestuous seas so well?
Can written word evoke or seascape paint
The fury, find elsewhere some parallel?
He breathes with us the Hebridean air
And lingers, though his body isn't there.

The Fate of Fine Art

Too late to turn the clock back on fine art,
Egregious oxymoron that it may
Be called today, but where to find the start
Of this, the slow beginnings of decay?

For once we found our world inside the space
That we saw bounded by a frame. The height
Of charm resided in the commonplace
Where now the commonplace is merely trite.

And in that world we knew the things we felt,
We recognised, the life we saw and thought
We knew, the things we touched and heard and smelt
And learned and read,
the things that we'd been taught.

And then it seems the Fauvist movement came
Along, divorcing outline, colour, shade
And form, each from the other. Should we blame
Matisse, for one, the hotchpotch he portrayed?

Technique and skill no longer score in art,
Nor presentation. Concept counts for all.
When craft in execution lost its part
For art it proved the writing on the wall.

Today's *great* works of art are meant to shock,
Are often vulgar, utterly debased,
Designed to ape the loathsome, out to mock
The twee and every benchmark of good taste.

The more ephemeral a work of art,
Like children's castle carvings in wet sand,
The greater chance that it will fall apart,
The higher price it seems it will command.

Artists today will brush aside our fears
Of transience. They've no concern, at heart,
For what effect will have the passing of the years
On shoddy work and shoddy works of art.

Long gone the days when artists would have ground
And bound their own pigments, who had the sense
To choose the methods that they found were sound
While having due regard to permanence.

No more can art astound us or confound
Our visual acuity or raise
Perceptions and our awe, where once we found
That it would open up our eyes, amaze

Us, make us look and look again in ways
We couldn't see till artists lent their sight
To us and then on nature we would gaze
Anew to see more clearly in the light.

As poetry today must be opaque,
Have scant regard for scansion, feet or rhyme,
So too in art the rules that we can break
Can only lead to anarchy in time.

A bandwagon for those without restraint,
A permit to create without constraint,
A licence to bespatter, daub and taint
Their canvases with cheap emulsion paint.

Too late to rescue art from all the wrong
Publicity it draws, the ridicule,
Perplexity and disbelief along
With scorn for what shows not a minuscule

Amount of talent or ability.
The cutting edge of art today is all
About sensation and celebrity
And arrogance, audacity and gall.

It shows how far the talentless can stretch
The boundaries of what they're able to:
Some wretch can spend five minutes on a sketch
That ends up as a seminal breakthrough

For vorticist post-futuristic art.
An etching smaller than a postage stamp
In fetching multi-squillions, apart
From all the kudos for the little scamp,

It gets his latest retrospective flown
To all the seven continents and sent
Off to the Venice Biennale, shown
At every single pseudo-art event.

Why paint a portrait of a man and try
To catch his likeness if you can? Just do
A daub with jumbo dung and let it dry,
Entitle it "Untitled, Number Two."

If only artists could just stand apart
From flagrant self-advertisement and hype
And put more effort into so-called art
They'd churn out ten times more appalling tripe.

"Laudamus te"

From J S Bach's B minor Mass

This aria so beautifully sung,
Its obbligato part ethereal;
Such coloratura from one so young,
So evanescent, immaterial.
Her limpid voice would almost somersault,
While dancing back and forth in swift ascent
Until it seemed to reach the heavens' vault,
The very portals of the firmament.

But someone else sang in the choir that day,
Our happiness Bach's music might have sealed.
I cared for her far more than I could say,
With choral music our belovèd field:
That lass at mass alas I said I'd wed
She'd lief have read my requiem instead.

George Frideric Handel

With Henry Purcell England's music died,
Till Handel graced our god-forsaken shores.
In retrospect a cause for loud applause,
One nation's loss recovered England's pride.
So many operas composed beside
His sacred choral work, his music soars
Beyond the stratosphere and underscores
His genius for God is at his side.

At trumpet blast the cymbals' crash; profound
The thunder of the drums; from mellow sound
His baton draws the hautboys' squealing tone.
Recorders pipe their shrill notes overblown.
While he conducts he doesn't stand alone
For God is with him and God loves His own.

Jimi Hendrix

Next door did rock star Jimi Hendrix dwell,
Whose stardom left him in a purple haze
Of drug abuse. Societal malaise
And good intentions paved his road to hell.
His drugs were recreational, the smell
Of LSD would send him tripping, raise
The roof in ways he never dreamt, to craze
The mind and extirpate the brain as well.

Had Handel shared his century might they
Have shared his music, Handel flaunting, say,
His cocked hat, great-coat, hose, full-bottomed wig,
And Hendrix in his Levis on a gig?
Great epics from the bible not his scene:
How fortunate those long years intervene.

George Stubbs's "Cheetah and Stag with Two Indians"

It's difficult to understand today
How virtuous propriety could go
To such extremes. Victorians aglow
With rectitude and sentiment would say,
"Why *did* George Stubbs so tastelessly portray
The stag and cheetah in the same tableau?"
So cruel, in such propinquity, to show
The mighty hunter and its feeble prey.

The stag it was they simply painted out,
Merged with its background, now restored to view.
But we are worse than they without a doubt,
We care not what we put our livestock through:
The slaughterhouse is hidden from our sight.
And makes it easy to ignore their plight.

Salvador Dali in Glasgow

While some protest too much, methinks a few
(Of those who metaphorically smear
Their excrement about as infants do
While overcompensating for their sheer
Incompetence with paint to use abstract
Expressions, half-baked, meaningless and backed
By arty claptrap, brazen eye contact)
Think they convincingly refute the fact.

Art isn't dead, perhaps, but moribund.
Post nineteen hundred this, and I am stunned
To find Dali could paint so well I see:
So free of decadence, so masterly,
Such chiaroscuro and fine brushwork done
As recently as nineteen fifty-one!

Salvador Dali's "Christ of Saint John of the Cross"

I

This picture shrieks with silent anguish. Racked
With pain, belied by bloodless hands and feet;
Intolerable torments, they compete
As muscles in that arching back contract.
His hanging head forestalls all eye contact;
And here we see Him, harrowing complete,
As Pilate meted out from judgment seat
Beyond this lorn forsaken barren tract.

And Dali gives us stage lighting to show
These youthful figures tinctured gold below,
Are simple fishermen. And there they stand,
Aghast at what they cannot understand:
For Christ the Son of God exalted some
To share His state and close to Him become.

II

Beneath their feet they furl a fishing net,
These figures that we see upon the ground.
Twilight, a nightjar makes its urgent sound
Unseen, a distant double bark offset
By otherwise persistent silence. Yet
Wherewith is this scene lit? The black profound
Above, behind us to our left, all round
Embrowned, kaleidoscopic colours set

To raze the parchèd earth. And these young men
Would never know a jeunesse dorée then,
They flung their nets, repaired them when required,
They ate when hungry, slept when they were tired:
But here we see, their garments flecked with gold,
These young ones mark the new as we the old.

III

How can His body hang, no nails to hands
Or feet as Dali has Him here portrayed?
So anodyne this bloodless corpse, conveyed
To blackest heights above the barren lands
Of Israel: the dreadful pain demands
Our awe, the horror that is here betrayed,
That dead weight tortured angle still displayed,
Such agony an infant understands.

But this is not a Cranach and nor yet
A Grünewald. We are not moved today
By horrors that were suffered yesterday.
Inured to Bosch and Brueghel scenes of sweat
And pain more present horrors that we dread:
The pickled shark and that revolting bed.

IV

How sad to see around us decadence
On such a scale there is no turning back,
No slightest evidence that common sense,
Can any more prevail against attack.
We cannot ever get back what we had
And there is no return to where we were,
The world's artistic cognoscenti mad:
Dali the last hope of the connoisseur?

For he could paint, with sable in his hand.
Only in trompe l'œil is there a demand
That we suspend our disbelief, it's good
His two dimensions keep his art surreal:
In Emin's bed, Quinn's head of frozen blood
The horror and the nastiness are real.

"Faithful unto Death"
Sir Edward John Poynter

From Parthenope's coast each to his post,
Beseeching eyes upraised with steady gaze.
That night would nature's cruelty erase
A city from the broiling earth and roast
The dying with the lying dead. Utmost
The pain, the choking pyroclastic haze
Whose toxic clouds cloak rivers all ablaze,
Each supplicating cast its living ghost.

The courage of the fearful soars beyond
The reckless resignation of the blind.
Vesuvius: our fears today still correspond
With his the way two thousand years behind
Our time, recorded on a water clock,
These seething seas met solid streaming rock.

Ordure or Dürer

Purely since they protest too much, methinks,
They wink while mixing pigments, dyes and inks
With excrement, to make a colour that
Was furnished by their next-door neighbour's cat.

So ill-advised it is, don't compromise
The tinting strength of pigments in this guise.
Just like the bitumen that Reynolds tarred
His pictures with, it only dries as hard.

Tat hangs on walls, it's never built to last.
Painters today learn nothing from the past.
Client and conservator, lord and liege
Extend longevity while under siege.

Few met Stanley Spencer, and fewer met
His friends. They might have been far fewer yet
If they'd let him use more colonic paint:
Spread thinly as his blusterous PR ain't.

Mix engraving ink, deep black for mezzotint,
Fine rosin powder for an aquatint,
With burins useless in the hands of fools.
Not Dürer though: he'd never blame his tools.

Mute buttons would be perfect to assail
The critics of our artistic travail,
The use of elephant and badger dung
Demands a clothes' peg or a nasal bung.
Ignore the smell (you can't) as you disrobe:
You'll find it's coming from the werderobe.

Note: *The first and last few letters of each stanza give*
different words for dung: pure, scat, soil, shard,
tath, siege, fewmets, spraint, mixen, stools, mute,
buttons, werderobe.

The Classical and the Gothic

If Queen Victoria were ever made to choose
Between the sorts of building prevalent
And motifs used for their embellishment,
What styles of architecture would enthuse?
"Deeside gives we," says she, "Such stonking views
A belvedere we'd think was heaven-sent.
But would a vine-scroll running ornament
Fuse Scots baronial and Gothic mews?"

Though mixing Gothic and Renaissance forms
Might certainly dispense with all the norms,
With egg-and-dart in trefoils round the gable
We're still unable to afford a stable.
Our master bedroom horses have abused:
We try to tell them, "We are not amused."

"Mariana"
Sir John Everett Millais

Aweary she, of waiting constantly,
Of waiting long for one who never comes.
Her lamentations piteous to see,
But he will not return and she succumbs
To languor and she wishes she were dead.
"Five long and lonely years I've lingered here,
Inside this moated grange," worn out, she said.
"He won't return, he'll not come back I fear."

Look closely at her window in the grange:
That casement can't be opened from within.
The room unswept, the sycamore, how strange,
How did it shed so many leaves therein?
Though leaves may enter none can leave the room,
Nor broom can sweep leaves from a sealèd tomb.

"The Hireling Shepherd"
William Holman Hunt

This comely wench was Emma Watkins, she
Who sat for Hunt in eighteen fifty-two.
Too unaffected she, she never knew
What lay beyond the brink, beyond the lee
Of innocence. Nor could she ever see
The fame at second hand that would accrue
Through all who gazed upon her face anew
As through Hunt's perfect eye so too do we.

And hers a kind of immortality,
Her face from fate's obscurity set free,
And better known though dead is she, so too,
Is every ewe and every tree we see
More living still than Hunt, known chiefly through
His art and such as Emma's buxom view.

"Proserpine"
Dante Gabriel Rossetti

Empress of Hades and a goddess she,
Unwilling bride to Pluto here she stands,
And in the left of her beseeching hands
She bears the fruit she'd taken from the tree.
Her mother Ceres' importunity
Led her to make of Jupiter demands
That Pluto should return her to the lands
Of Terra Mater and to set her free.

If only she had known a single seed
Of that forbidden fruit would sadly lead
To this dark cloister, looking furtively
Through Hades' window at the sullen sky,
Nor quite enough to turn night here to day
Nor dark enough to let her slip away.

2 High Seas on Hebrid Isles

Spring

In spring the crocuses broke out as bold
As brass from refuge in their barren clay.
They speared the air in colourful array
And blazoned they their petals proudly told
Of azure and of purpure and of gold.
Heraldic, seméed in a field were they,
Where cultivated gardens may display
New growth and hopes unfurl amid the old.

How numinous the force that can roll out
Rich carpets over seeming fruitless drought!
Our humble task, to give each plant a name:
Fireweed perhaps, or rosebay willowherb?
We curb the weed, the herb we don't disturb:
But in His eyes they surely are the same.

Summer

High summer now, the rambling hedgerows loud
With magpies' urgent rattle; thorny nest
In hawthorn long abandoned, now possessed
By creeping things, new leaves their living shroud.
In season's thunderstorms and heavy cloud,
Well hidden in the deepest thicket best
Permits the shrew some fitful sort of rest,
From snake and stoat the only sort allowed.

The turpentine seen bleeding from the pine:
The deathcap; hemlock, poisons' archetype;
And bursting forth forbidden fruit, a sign
Of all that's cloying, fulsome, over-ripe.
And Adam ate whatever Eve would bring,
Beguiled he was, he ate of everything.

Autumn

In Eden's garden rampant weeds were found,
Disease and blight on every fruit and flower,
Near leafless they and lifeless every bower,
The broad oaks' welcome shadows now surround
The garden walls, in harsh white half-light bound.
Beneath the louring naked hills they cower,
The raindrops sour that fall in storm and shower,
Well-trodden through the sodden peaty ground.

The birds have flown, the swallow and the swift;
Beginning their transcontinental drift
The martins from their cradles in the eaves.
The thorns still barb the rose that's shed its leaves,
But soon we'll hear the hardy redwing sing
Through winter bringing promise of the spring.

Winter

In winter clarity is best of all,
Cerulean-bright the sky or Wedgwood blue
Revealing frosted cobwebs in the dew.
The ice creeps slowly over all to sprawl
In sculpted drapes on frozen waterfall,
Shapes Michelangelo could no more hew
Than cast in bronze the wizened churchyard yew
Or bring to life the sightless in their pall.

And in the shortest days our menfolk brawl
For when the nights are long their tempers fray.
The women call for peace, their children bawl,
The old become more bitter by the day.
For young and old the days are bitter cold
And each cold night more bitter for the old.

The Evacuation of St Kilda

No idyll did he shatter nor could he,
The early tourist, wealth at his command,
Unless grey stones lapped by a freezing sea
Make sunless Tartarus the promised land.
Their life was harsh, so they with passing grief
Four thousand years of history resigned
And for a better land, to their relief,
They left a bleak and dismal world behind.

Their ship hove to, no dogs allowed on deck.
Hopes dashed with heavy stones around each neck
They drowned their dogs, and next day far and wide
Their bodies lay above the ebbing tide.
In Village Bay they drowned their dogs: the day
They were aweigh they drowned them in the bay.

Rockall

In nineteen fifty-five claimed for the Queen,
A sea-girt rock so far away from land,
It isn't difficult to understand
Exactly why it's scarcely ever seen
And why so very few have ever been.
Could anybody really take command
Of such a dreary granite rock, to stand
Upon the single feature in between

The summit ridge and sea below? Hall's Ledge
Is flat enough for guillemots to stop.
But see its narrow width and view the edge:
The wind is fierce, vertiginous the drop,
No halcyon days to quell the swell, too steep
This granite hump, the seas too hellish deep.

Gruinard Island

Remote it lies from any tourist trail,
Albeit barely half a mile offshore.
It holds a secret dating from the war,
A proving ground behind the darkest veil
Of night, for evil such as this must quail
Before the glaring light of day, before
The gagging press-hounds baying at the door,
Before the sight of God and on a scale

Beyond the pale today? If only it
Were so! Those anthrax trials we deplore
Where now we can with just a single hit
Annihilate the human race and more:
Beneath the heavens' vault a sombre shroud,
Still swathes Gruinard today in blackest cloud.

The Flannan Isles

Upon the storm-lashed Flannan Isles one grey
December hour, while still the night, these three
Young lighthousemen had breakfast; tidily
They piled the plates and put the pots away.
The light was out, the hearth-stone chill and they
Had gone, and on the mantel plain to see
The clock had stopped at three. Where could they be
But in the sea, how had they gone astray?

The stories flew around but no-one knew
What happened to the sturdy lighthouse crew
For they were never seen again. What doom
Befell them in the gloom, those three for whom
The light went out that wintry night forlorn
Who sought the morn that never brought the dawn?

North Rona

Remote his fortress, far from humankind
And girt by thirteen leagues of open sea,
Was Rona's lonely hermit ever free
To contemplate, forsake the daily grind
And find the time to discipline the mind?
He strove with nature's forces gallantly,
Fought elemental strife he couldn't flee,
Nor could he leave his earthly cares behind.

As Francis tamed the wolf, as Gall enthralled
The bear, as Cuthbert in his wisdom called
The otters from the sea, so Ronan must
Have loved the seals and won their loyal trust,
For still they feed and breed around the coast,
On vigil through the night the Holy Ghost.

The Wreck of the Annie Jane

Beneath this barren strand on Vatersay
Are all at rest I trust where we have lain
Through storm and thunder, hail and sleet and rain.
Four hundred and some fifty sailed away,
A hundred lived, we others died that day
In eighteen fifty-three when Annie Jane,
Dismasted in a storm, could not maintain
Her errant course and foundered in the bay.

En route from Liverpool to Montreal
We drowned, they buried us close by the shore.
No longer do our dying children call,
There's peace in this pale earth forevermore
For there's a fellow comfort in our graves,
Awash at times with gently lapping waves.

3 Mountains

&

Mountaineers

Climbing the Weisshorn

It seems like yesterday the day we stood
Below its long east ridge. I call to mind
Our youth, how gratified we were to find
The top came sooner than we thought it could.
The climb belied its aspect, how it should
Have gone, the icy ridge so well defined
It eased the way, as though it were designed
To lead us there in safety as it would.

But that was forty years ago, before
The ill-spent years. Though sorely we deplore
A vanished youth, from summit to the slough,
A futile life is hard to disavow.
While youth is wasted on the young it's said
It's useless to the agèd and the dead.

An Unlikely Meeting

Some twenty years ago its even slope,
From Ngauruhoe's crater came in sight.
With gentle gradient and modest height
Mount Ruapehu never could give scope
For climbing with an ice-axe and a rope.
But having reached its summit in half light
A man approached, so sprightly that he might
Have been an ibex or an antelope.

And strange to say, twelve thousand miles away,
His brother lived just three from me, a day
And night in flight from us. Though long ago
The Greeks had spanned the world does it still grow
As scientists maintain? The more we think
We know this earth the more it seems to shrink.

Toni Kurz

Those frozen hours he hanged: so inhumane
At twenty-three, the death of Toni Kurz.
The image on that page still reasserts
His long slow dying through the night. In vain
Can photographs like this our grief contain!
Some eighty years have passed and still it hurts,
But pity youth itself for their deserts
Are all in prospect, some in ghastly pain.

To climb the nordwand of the Eiger it
Requires the courage of a tiger, fit
But prudent too. And don't rely upon
Brute force or youth alone as Kurz had done:
Technique is all for should we lose our grip
The first may well become our final slip.

Climbers of Kathmandu

Around the airport lounge in Kathmandu
The tourist in his fake designer gear
Is scoffed at by the pukka mountaineer,
While those with more street cred than sense make do
With Gucci handbags, shoes by Jimmy Choo.
Much less well-dressed and less impressed each year
The rats have neither boots nor socks to wear
But they could teach us all a thing or two

About survival, self-denial and
What truly matters in our petty lives.
It's very difficult to understand
Why one who climbs, and doesn't need to, strives
To stay alive through self-imposed ordeal,
Achieving goals both pointless and unreal.

An Accident on Mount Fuji

These harmless slopes, in winter snow they could
Be witness to such accidents. His fall,
Three thousand feet, was followed by a crawl,
Two hundred yards on ice and frozen mud.
Five broken bones, brain haemorrhage, a good
Few bruises and an eye beyond recall.
That seven-hour search found him at last and all
But dead. They took some photos where they stood.

Those photos, of a battered corpse they first
Took him to be, for they'd foreseen the worst.
One finds it strangely unaffecting though,
That bloody trail seen weaving in the snow:
Of his abrupt descent he's unaware,
Could that be me? I surely wasn't there.

Moonraker

At Berry Head in Devon is a climb
That fiercely overhangs its shadowed base
By many yards across the sea. With prime
Location, fearsome aspect and its face
All swathed in darkness, chilly as a tomb,
Moonraker, though not classed among "extremes,"
Sustains its hardships mounting in the gloom
On tiny holds and hubris, so it seems.

As near to hell as one may find on earth,
A Bosch forsaken by its fiends, yet made
That place a horror long before their birth.
And then at last above the Stygian shade,
A clifftop bright with sunlight, joyous sight,
Of flasks and hampers, children in delight.

An Ascent of Mont Blanc

Three days from Manchester the summit gained,
The highest in the Alps, a chilly spot;
Attaining it no strain if I had trained
For it, a migraine pain as I had not.
For scientific ends it was first scaled
With great long-handled axes and true grit,
Hemp ropes, and climbing boots
well waxed and nailed,
They weren't just there to make a day of it.

That's testified by all the plonk they brought,
Red noses from the beaujolais they drank,
Champagne and burgundy, sack, hock and port.
For Dutch courage they had the schnapps to thank.
(To vaunt their strictly academic sphere
They also took some barometric gear.)

The Chudleigh Overhang

Neglected now are Chudleigh Rocks: we used
To scale these Devon crags while students there.
With creeping moss and ivy now unclear,
Bold routes that inexplicably enthused
Us then some forty years ago, amused
Us risking life and limb by flouting fear
And gravity. Sheer rock it had and here
It was: with oozing palms and fingers bruised

We soloed Chudleigh Overhang. Without
A rope or helmet, wearing bovver boots,
It seemed a brutish thing without a doubt
To climb, and harder than so many routes.
But why, with life and prospects then so dear,
Were we in retrospect so cavalier?

A Piano on Ben Nevis

Ben Nevis, and the tallest Scottish hill,
We clambered up the first time fifty years
Ago as children, and with all the thrill
And derring-do of alpine pioneers.
But bringing us both down to earth we saw
A man ahead of us upon the track,
And stumbling upward painfully he bore
The weight of a piano on his back.

On our descent he'd gained but little height,
Was little further on from Achintee,
But was it just a trick of early light
That morning or his bid for charity,
That bearded in the mist he looked to me
For all the world like Christ on Calvary?

Trekking up Kilimanjaro

How dull and tedious it was, its height
Deceives, it's still a hill, and though it's tall
Its profile's so familiar to all,
Why fly to Tanzania for a sight
Of it? Unprepossessing lump and quite
Harmless, its slopes could scarce hold one in thrall,
No knife-edge ridge or craggy peak or wall
Of hanging ice to gird its awesome might.

And yet it has its charms in some degree:
The bracing windswept yomp across the moor;
The end at last of all that bloody scree;
Gasping at the scenery; the summit tour;
And just before precipitate retreat,
To have a continent beneath our feet.

Crowded Moments

Around those crowded moments in our lives
The deepest fog may linger year on year.
But climbing high the memory revives
As forest, scrub and pasture disappear.
Above the clouds bare rock and ice, on seas
Peach-tinted islands glow. In times misspent
On mountains it's the summits that appease
Us for the tiresome labours of ascent.

Above the cloud an icy realm, the home
Of chough and swift and vast Laputas borne
Aloft: the Weisshorn, Obergabelhorn,
The Dent Blanche, Zinalrothorn and the Dom,
Their cornices from forty years ago
When held in mind still feel as bright as snow.

Climbing the Matterhorn

Near fifteen thousand feet above the sea
Though from afar the Matterhorn stands proud
It earns respect no longer from the crowd
That crawl upon its blackened ice and scree.
Unstable rocks dislodged by some we see
Past caring for restraint among those bowed
With clanking gear, an early morning shroud
Concealing climbers and their gaucherie.

We don't defeat these mountains on their first
Ascent or conquer them or at the worst,
Like braggarts, "knock the bastards off" as did
Ed Hillary, lest modesty forbid.
The mountains are aloof. They merely choose
To lend us their perspective and their views.

Edward Whymper

A man obsessed might Edward Whymper be,
In his determination to succeed.
With rugged looks in rugged Harris tweed,
And with his trusty axe he'd never flee.
With: "Quand j'emploi ce piolet," for me
His single-mindedness was guaranteed,
He carved it on his axe and there we read,
(Ironic this) "J'ai toujours réussi."

Among the greatest in the Alps, the last
To yield. Four fellow-climbers fell aghast,
The mountain won for they came off the worst.
Those tangled limbs and mangled bodies burst,
Their smile stillborn. A mile or more that morn
These four men measured on the Matterhorn.

In Praise of the Nepalese Rat

The rats infesting Kathmandu Airport
Appear to co-exist in peace with man
And have, it seems, since local time began,
Been treated each like some great Juggernaut.
Their teeming numbers give no pause for thought
To thwart the airport staff: it seems they can
Induce distinct responses other than
Our atavistic dread and fears self-taught.

For no-one here will blench at sight of them,
They take these lowly creatures in their stride,
Perhaps admire them for their stolid phlegm,
Insouciance, and valiance. Beside
The threat of warfarin or shotgun blast
Their nonchalance you'll find is unsurpassed.

George Mallory

Could there have been a flimsier pretext
For his attempt at self-aggrandisement,
This figure, brave, anti-establishment,
Whose disappearance left the world perplexed?
For he climbed Everest, and though it vexed
Us all for many years, the labour spent
On finding if he finished his ascent,
No-one can really say what happened next.

As he climbed out of sight into the mist
The rest is mystery. Who could resist
His famous words that constantly recur:
He climbed the mountain just "Because it's there."
These ill-judged words this worthy sage manqué
So wisely said then staggered on his way.

Sir Edmund Hillary

What kind of arrogance asserts that we
Have conquered Everest? For still it stands,
Unbowed and proud. It won't be at our hands
Should all this scree and glacial debris
And snow and ice be dashed into the sea.
No flaccid armchair mountaineer commands
Such knowledge of the Khumbu, understands
As he how hanging seracs held the key;

That siege tactics avail to scale its height;
Toes lost to frostbite; snowblind, some to fight
Exhaustion, reaching higher into space.
The mountain, though, would still take pride of place
If he'd not climbed it with the Nepalese
But stayed at home attending to his bees.

The Rats of Kathmandu

At Kathmandu Airport are rats much-sought
As marvellous examples of the way
Two species live in harmony today
In symbiotic union, in short.
Though fancied for their fur sometimes, or bought
For fancy breakfast fare, we always say
We're grateful to the rodents we betray.
Relationships indeed are seldom fraught.

The rats are often kept as friends or pets,
Inoculated by the local vets;
They feed upon the fattest cats they find
Combined with fag ends, bats and bacon rind;
And leave their faecal footprints on the ground,
The runway and the tarmac all around.

A Climbing Accident
in Cornwall

His eyes alone were screaming in his fall,
Directed towards me or something way
Beyond us both and pleading on that day
That silently he fell. He made no call
To me for help nor could I hear at all,
Above the ruthless crashing sea, the stray
Gulls laughing mercilessly in the bay
On winds that lashed Bosigran's granite wall.

Head furthest from the crag he passed from sight,
His legs out straight, arms stretched as
though he might
Be hanging from the cross, his fatal due
For worldly joys so pitifully few?
Would he extend his end beyond his birth
Could he portend how life would end on earth?

An Incident on the Cornish Cliffs

So many things were churning in his mind
When scrambling down the track towards the cove,
To take especial care or drop behind
Them both, decide perhaps it might behove

Him to feign injury before his friends,
Avert the worst accurst day of his life,
Reverse his steps, the coward who intends
To yield before a hint of mental strife?

The voices in his head said "No, don't go,
For this is bluster, braggadocio,
And sheer bravado, putting on a show
For those below, as you must surely know.

The subjugation of your Everest
Does little to augment the sum of joy
On earth, no greater for your vain conquest
Nor growth in health nor wealth will we enjoy."

A self-indulgence this can only be,
Though steeped in needless fears and
pointless dread,
The footpath led the way through rock debris,
The boulders all around them widely spread.

His friends, oblivious to fearful thought,
To nagging pains he felt deep down inside
His very core of being. Quite distraught
Was he beneath his overweening pride.

But credence he could scarcely ever give
To vague portentous hints, unwonted fears,
For dreams should not dictate the way we live
Nor night-time sorrows turn our days to tears.

And down the track three climbers made their way,
Between the granite boulders, heaps of stone,
And one of them would die that fateful day
Who climbed with two but sadly died alone.

He died alone that fateful day. He died
For no more reason than his self-esteem,
For nothing but that vain and arrant pride,
Could engineer fulfilment of his dream.

Too late by far for any to beseech
Them now. They raced, ignoring their sixth sense,
In haste to reach that great impending breach
That faced them and their misplaced confidence.

A bowline held the gear around each waist,
The crag grew near and one of them felt queer,
Too late by now to leave the wall disgraced.
No matter for these climbers would appear

Externally too very cavalier
To dread a fall. But one of them was full
Of fright that fateful day and fighting fear,
The hidden terror pounding in his skull.

He led the route straight up though with a lack
Of holds on fist-jams with the odd layback,
The tiniest of ledges let him pack
Two wedges in an overhanging crack.

And on pitch three he climbed above a nose
Of rock obtruding three yards into space,
With holds scarce big enough for twinkletoes
To grip the wrinkles of its granite face.

A micro-wedge gave little confidence
Jammed in the most exiguous of cracks,
Protection of such little consequence,
No spot to waver, nowhere to relax.

Towards a faint handhold he made a lunge,
The movement let his quaking foot slip free,
The wedge sprang out, he took a mighty plunge,
His arms outspread, his head towards the sea.

He made no shout to us nor flailed about
Nor scrabbled hopelessly, but seemed subdued,
For nothing could avail him now without
The kindly intercession of Saint Jude.

He made no shout, an utter waste of breath
For nobody could save him from this grim,
Inevitable imminence of death,
Nor time had he to make his peace with Him.

No help for it, he plummeted earthbound,
A hundred feet he fell without a sound
To hit the rocks and debris on the ground,
The gulls abounding, laughing all around.

And still they laughed and wheeled about and still
Their raucous screams, unchecked by all they'd seen,
Crescendoed with a will, the air they'd fill
With shrieks and cries and everything between.

The gulls were gliding in their element
And floating on the thermals high above.
Their capabilities are heaven-sent
And shared by auk and petrel, hawk and dove,

But not by man nor any of his kind,
To avian propensities unknown,
For unpowered flight was never man designed
As Icarus and Daedalus had shown.

Three climbers on this Cornish cliff, one dead,
And two forever chastened by his fall.
Forever both were filled with awful dread,
So cowed were they before that granite wall.

And surely better had he not been born,
The bliss of twenty years unmissed? Had he
Foreknowledge of that brutal end forlorn
Would he have begged to be or not to be?

His stricken partners on the crag no more
Could reach him than could soothe his dying groans
As he lay helpless on the shingle shore,
His shattered bones among the broken stones.

4 Places Famous
&
Forgotten

At Machu Picchu

From Aguas Calientes the ride ends
At Machu Picchu on a battered bus
That takes us via countless hairpin bends
Up to the top then leaves the site to us.
We aimlessly infest each empty home,
Each roofless shell and every grass-grown heap,
Where ghosts of fifteenth century Inca roam,
And tourists dream or cogitate or sleep.

On our return to Aguas down the track
And cutting every corner was the sound
Of youths who'd race our bus the whole way back.
And when they won they'd pass a hat around.
How enterprising were those boys to see
This honest means of dunning you and me?

In Trafalgar Square

Sublime he looks, majestic as he should,
With bicorn, sash and ceremonial sword,
At fifty metres high his pillar would
Knock any stylite off his perch. Restored,
His stately statue looks so proud above
The seething mass of pigeons far below,
The people, cars and heady fumes thereof
Enough to give bold Nelson vertigo.

With lofty thoughts so nobly does he stand
Above pedestrian minds, he's so well-bred
But rather less commanding, less than grand,
The worthy Nelson loses all street cred
When seagulls spot a handy landing and
Evacuate their bowels on his head.

Kinlochresort, Harris

The distance nearly eight miles from the south
Across the bleak and trackless Harris moor,
Much easier from Loch Resort's broad mouth
By boat from its remote Atlantic shore.
The settlement abandoned long ago,
Yet there an old man and his dog we saw,
He standing motionless, his head below
The ancient lichened lintel of his door.

He stood in reverie. And there we sat
Apart, no tritely spoken words that might
Invade his solitude, his habitat
And one-time home. It somehow seemed not right
In such a lorn sequestered place to breach
The silence with banalities of speech.

Reinigeadal, Harris

So many years ago it was, a child
Tramped up from East Loch Tarbert's rocky shore
Across the peat haggs underneath the wild
And dismal sky that overhung the moor.

No road could lead him thence, a mere track
Between the heather clumps, it weaved its way
Through crumbling gneiss, the acid bistre-black
And clotted earth its peaty overlay.

And though remote a little school was there
Some three miles distant from the nearest road,
Too late, it closed before, as all elsewhere,
They reaped the blessings that a road bestowed.

For then across the open moor abloom
With gorse it ran, hard-core laid down and sealed,
A hostel, no plush inn for those for whom
Upon a whim the "spartan" life appealed.

Their isolation over, though for some
The road had ended rather more than this;
Our senses sharpened in detachment from
The mass, so much in aggregate we miss.

Those few would say a price too much to pay,
Such highways to salvation they disdain,
Inured to penury and pain as they,
To constant mist and constant driving rain.

The hermit life can bring us some degree
Of inner peace with independence, hence,
Resourcefulness and self-sufficiency
With self-reliance and resilience.

We find out who we are and need to be
If we're alone or nearly on our own,
We learn to cope outside our colony
And how to live without a mobile phone.

How hard sometimes in such a hostile land,
No company, forsaken by our kind,
In storm-force wind and sleet, to understand
Just what *is* with intelligence designed?

And then we must believe this life to be
A proving ground, though still the Western Isles
With much that seems inimical, agree
They're happier than we despite their trials.

For they are closer to the land and sea,
Less trammelled by association with
Their fellow man's complexities, and free
To dwell on past times, ancestry and myth.

To sense the land anew each day they touch
It with a stranger's hand, see with the eyes
Of children microcosms, letting such
Creations bring them wonder and surprise.

In minute intricacies we can find
Within a feather, leaf or powdered wing
Of butterfly or moth the mastermind
Behind the life and soul of everything.

As children may with wonderment acquire
Of astronomical extremities
In counting grains of sand at Luskentyre
A tiny hint of their immensities.

And closer to the numinous are we
Atop a Harris hill than ever he
In any Harris kirk on bended knee
On any sabbath day can ever be.

A dismal sky still overhangs the moor
Today where years ago it was that he
Tramped up from East Loch Tarbert's rocky shore
Across the peat haggs from a cold grey sea.

Dundrennan Abbey

Here at Dundrennan Mary slept her last
Unfettered night then plied her course between
Bleak hope and ghastly dread, her future cast
Upon the mercy of a fickle queen.
To Solway at the Abbey Burn she came
Where on the shore the burbling rill still spills
Into the Firth. Nought else remains the same
Beyond the timeless profile of the hills.

Had she foreknown the horror of those years
That lay in prospect, nineteen years' despair,
Intrigue and vacillation, constant fears;
Would she have sailed, to seek through
tears or prayer,
Her cousin's intercession to relax
Those fears that culminated in the axe?

Molinginish, Harris

So bleak these shores, devoid of humankind.
Long derelict, abandoned; each old house
Now choked with blaeberry and ling, consigned
To wheatear, corncrake, sandpiper and grouse.
But one still roofed stood by the desert shore
And from a single hinge yet barely hung
And flapping to and fro its open door
Still back and forth all day and night it swung.

A home that grieved its desolation, cried
For warmth and wept for its neglect. Beside
Three penny coins upon the mantel lay
A pair of specs, mute relics that inveigh
Against their erstwhile owners' constant strife
Sustaining an intolerable life.

Browned off in Saddleworth

What can the tourists do in Uppermill?
For once they've fed the mallards on the green
And been to view St Chad's upon the hill
There's little in between they haven't seen.

But by the church are murder victims' bones,
Their case a cause célèbre at the time,
They lie beneath their lichened ledger stones,
Their souls at peace we hope, at heights sublime.

A cross from eighteen fifty-seven marks
The spot James Platt MP was shot and killed:
On stormy nights it's said his dog still barks
To rue a life of promise unfulfilled.

High on the crags existence was austere,
Flint arrowheads attest in gloomy caves;
Our hairy ancestors sequestered here
And festered in their shallow peaty graves.

Upon the moss our Mother Nature breathed,
The moor the lungs for many northern towns.
Two hundred years of sooty smoke once wreathed
Around and sheathed the scene in deepest browns.

Between his earthly toil and heavens' vault
A storm picked up the parson to ensure
With pirouette and pike and somersault,
And impure thoughts a landing most demure.

Through wind and rain his hat sat on the moor.
Astride the deepest bog for months before
It blew away, and there he was of course,
Beneath his hat, still sitting on his horse.

And reeling through the town of Uppermill
The Hooray Henries and their "Air Hair Lairs!"
In hostelries they'll only sup until
They've finished talking hairlessness and heirs.

While some wear skirts indoors and
some wear drawers,
Tweed suits, galoshes, Norfolk jackets go
So well with Barbours, de rigueur outdoors,
Though polyester shirts malapropos.

And some dress down and camouflage in brown
And smell of umber humus, acid laced.
A sturdy Purdey might restore the crown
Of elegance, decorum and good taste.

The Glorious Twelfth! It's time a hotshot got
The lot, a moorcock flock in one pot shot;
A four-bore mounted on a four-by-four
With foresight, backsight and a Labrador.

A sledgehammer to crack a nut you'll say,
Can heavy ordnance never win the day,
Avail the best way to assail the quail
And every type of snipe and water-rail?

The local ramblers have a leader who
Is scarce as fit as he was hitherto;
He's always getting lost, pellucid bluffs
Including "Here we ares" and "Sure enoughs …"

It's time to blow the gaffe on all the guff:
Nor fit nor phat he's full of huff and puff,
Career gone by before it has begun,
He's on the moor no more, his days are done.

His clumbers number many of his dogs.
They climb and clamber round the amber bogs,
In peaty turgid seas of umber brown.
They'll let you drown but never let you down.

A birder too, he hears the bird he'd like
To think he's heard, the kite a common sight.
In flight the twite might be the red-backed shrike
As all that's trite becomes quite recondite.

A crack shot he, his notoriety
And insobriety in every pub
Precludes his joining the Society
Of Nerdy Birders at the Twitchers' Club.

Round every peat hagg, and down every grough
Through colours tawny, sepia and buff
The ground is rough enough, though all downhill
As we head back to vibrant Uppermill.

The children scream, they want to let off steam,
Their grown-ups scoffing cakes and clotted cream.
We went to every tea-shop on the way
And all were open on Midsummer's Day

For talks at the museum on "Just why
The Lesser Crested Diggle Dragonfly
May have returned to Denshaw," so they say.
They pray, one day, the Dobcross osprey may

Come back the same way as the ruff and reeve.
Why are the pubs shut midnight Christmas Eve?
Where can we go? The RC church nearby
Is open, go and praise the Lord most high

Or wait here till the summer for the chance
To see the rushcart taken to St Chads,
Or see the morris men in merry dance,
Go gurning through a halter with the lads.

For all that's done is dun in Saddleworth,
And everything with umber peat embrowned.
The sallow grassland binds the shifting earth
And all that lives and festers in the ground.

What can the tourists do in Uppermill
Now that they've fed the mallards and they've seen
St Chad's, on finding every woollen mill
Downtown is brown and every village green?

A Meeting on the Moor

Still frozen rigid was the turf, the mist
The chill wind stirred to twirl about the tor.
Ice-choked the Dart a hollow trickle bore,
And on the moor the mist would wreathe and twist.
As through a shroud half seen and in its midst
And borne upon the wind above the tor
And of the sky was she, the mist she wore,
Her evanescent figure could exist

For him no longer than a fleeting thought.
Her face he'd always known, its fragile tint
Echoed the winter dawn, a soulful hint
In eyes that told of one of whom she sought
Some trace upon the moor. It could not last,
Unlike the mist, the moment quickly passed.

A Stormy Night

We fear the seas' illimitable vast
Abyssal depths but not the pallid moon,
Emerging from enveloping cocoon
In faintly lumined billows now held fast,
Wrapped in the veil of night in clouds amassed.
How delicately arabesques festoon
The wave-tips all with livid flecks bestrewn
While rollers crash with fury unsurpassed.

Selene hangs above, a masterpiece
Of stillness and detachment and of peace.
Insouciant, unconcerned, dégagé,
A quarter of a million miles away
So who would even glimpse the feeble flop
Should Mars's Mount Olympus blow its top?

The Saddleworth Moors

To the Memory of Keith Bennett
Victim of the Moors Murderers, Died 16th June 1964

The moorland gutters drain the weeping moss
From tussock clumps on nameless heights above.
Old mounds still mark the parish bounds and cross
The storm-drenched blanket mire, the peat whereof
Still holds his body fast where he was drowned.
The bog moss, bilberry and cotton grass
Surround him in the quiet earth, unfound
Forevermore deep in this black morass.

The moors, complicit in the silence since,
How could that innocent's short life evince
The bliss of heaven, any joy on earth
Make up for all the years beneath it, birth
Unasked for and a sodden grave to cheer
Him, cold and dismal, desolate and drear?

Archaeology in Egypt

If you should go to Luxor stand beside
A pylon, look above in every nook
And cranny, bright as any picture book.
It's underneath entablatures, beside
The weatherproof and well-primed underside
Of architraves. Don't ask how long it took
To paint these colours, hard to overlook:
They're brighter than a Luxor travel guide.

And could those craftsmen possibly retrieve
The past three thousand years could they believe
Their colours would be visible today?
Could Horus, carved nearby in solid granite
Conceive there would be room for him to stay
With seven billion people on the planet?

Roe Deer Spotted in Radcliffe

Radcliffe we don't tend to associate
Immediately with shy spry Cervidae
Although they are indigenous to high
Ground further north. We overestimate
Their independence to anticipate
A Bambi Chop House soon. While pigs might fly
These roe deer can't and never even try
To use a zebra crossing or a gate.

So what attracts the deer to Radcliffe now?
Tattoo parlours and chances here to top
Up tans, the sybaritic sacred cow?
Chaps' chit-chat in chip shop and betting shop,
You think they'll find nirvana here? They won't,
Unless the deer know something that we don't.

The Taj Mahal

Built to commemorate a love that died
Four hundred years ago, how sad to say
She never saw what we can see today.
Serenely does its massive bulk preside
Above a seeming swamp on every side,
The damp is almost palpable, the grey
Skies vaunt its marble whiteness; see the way
Each precious stone belies what lies inside.

No whited sepulchre, nor yet could all
The labours of those twenty thousand men
Still find what lies within this marbled hall,
Exquisite creatures never seen again:
No artifice or art could ever halt
These noble corpses rotting in their vault.

An Indian Elephant

On visiting Sri Lanka years ago
We hired an elephant and a mahout.
For pachyderms the local sights were nowt
To spout about, blasé are they although
His proboscideans he'd guide aglow
With pride and ride beside them, wouldn't shout
At them for fear a long prehensile snout
He had no doubt could deal a knockout blow.

While telling us his tales of Serendip
Just one of his subungulates could nip
Our ears off, tear us limb from limb,
Should he be so inclined upon a whim.
That docile beast, though over nine feet high
Would no more rip a man apart than fly.

The Empire State Building

Shreve, Lamb and Harmon built the Empire State
        Building, no paragon of Art Deco;
    By feet it beat the Chrysler to elate
    Its ovine architect below. They'd crow
With pride to think how only five had left
    The job for only five had fallen off,
    But those five left five families bereft.
    Did Mr Lamb acknowledge that or doff

    His cap at topping out, bestow on them
    The freedom of the observation deck?
    Fatalities would fill him full of phlegm.
He wouldn't think "That might have been *my* neck."
His hands were white and smooth, for he would own
        He never laid a stone upon a stone.

The Great Wall of China

The only man-made object visible
From outer space! Could anyone believe
Words so demonstrably derisible?
A factoid far from likely to deceive,
It gives a meagre and a hollow worth
To what is great beyond its local fame,
The *only* evidence of man on earth?
No trite remark despite the fulsome claim.

And this is where some fifteen years ago
We two first met and nearly froze below
The icy walls at Badaling. I know
The fog-veiled vault above us spoke of woe,
And, so it seemed to me, of choking breath,
Of freezing skies and of a poignant death.

The Ngorongoro Crater

Intrepid we for sleeping out that night,
Full well we felt this thin and flimsy sheet
Of canvas kept inside the broiling heat
Remaining with the quickly failing light;
But more than that our unpatrolled campsite,
Exposed to carnivores, we hoped replete,
With what was left of last week's kill to eat;
Tomorrow's prey would not be us tonight.

Next day, ignoring us, a fearsome sight,
Two wildebeest surrounded by the might
Of ten lions. As one would rake their sides
With claws on bloody paws on bloody hides
To bring them down, so *we* had bated breath,
While bovine brains belied their brush with death.

The Bishop's Garden

I

Each year stuffed in its gable would a wren
Rebuild its hooded cradle in the shed,
Its feathered bed at level with my head.
A tawny owl would daunt it now and then,
On soundless wings but never breach its den,
And everywhere the giant knotweed spread;
Unkempt the lawns and every flower bed
Bespoke the idleness of clergymen.

At dusk the bats would flit on wrinkled wing,
Ill-favoured things, if only they could sing!
They skim and scythe the air in copse and glade
And all is tranquil: only owls betray
The silence from their cobweb-hooded shade
And stir to mourn the peaceful night away.

II

So long neglected over all these years,
And now abandoned to capricious fate,
Last opened fifty years ago this gate
Frames nothing at a closer view that cheers
The adamantine soul or quells the tears
Pathetic fallacy may generate.
When ivy and convolvulus abate
Then even more persistent weed appears.

Inside the gate and scattered all around
And triffid-like the giant hogweed found
With all that's rooted in the earth at war.
The bishop's palace grounds are long and wide.
Lorn, overgrown and wild the woodland floor
Where reptiles and all creeping things abide.

III

I took our dog with me and never met
Another soul in five or six hours' wandering
Round greenfield sites and farmland in the spring;
And from the soil I'd reap rare finds and let
The dog fetch many more. All worthless, yet
To one with fertile mind that twisted thing
Becomes a sixteenth century signet ring,
A linchpin for a landau, brooch beset

With bling. Where goldcrest and the bullfinch nest
Despondent thoughts would find me so distressed
Sometimes I swore I'd climb the highest elm
In transit to some awful godless realm,
And step out on the slimmest limb unsound
Earthbound, some eighty feet above the ground.

IV

I hoped my nerve would overwhelm for me
The terror in the falling and the pain:
I could not climb back down that tree again.
The shortest route of all to amnesty
Would need a moment's courage I could see,
The courage of a man with fevered brain,
The courage of one driven half insane.
To climb that blameless tree would need in me

More of a man than I could ever be.
Though I was driven nearly round the bend
This tree was not the way for me to flee,
No one-way ticket to a weary end.
How does it feel to die? It's hard for me
To tell you, lying dead beside a tree.

V

I'd hoped the height would overwhelm the pain,
I never could descend that elm again.
But sombre moods would change and I could be
As happy as a sandboy by the sea.
It might be Phoebus breaking through the cloud
Or lifting from some field its morning shroud,
Or bouncing off the bishop's righteousness
To galvanise the bishop's diocese.

Or yet the prospect of reed warblers' eggs
Well hidden there between riparian legs,
The beer-cans and the fag-ends in the sedge,
Though these might drive me very near the edge.
For nothing makes me feel more bitter than
The way that needless piles of litter can.

VI

The bishop's garden was in such a state
With may trees bending underneath the weight
Of magpies' thorny baskets reaching from the side
Of stagnant ponds; and crawling off to hide,
And under every stone a nether world
Of horror, pallid creatures lying curled
In sallow bloodless half-life loth to stay
And loth to drag their evil slime away.

And sure it is they had no earthly right
Those loathsome creatures in their horrid plight
To be, no right had they to nauseate
My sight while they await a gruesome fate.
In dying they let other pond life thrive,
Surviving death as when they were alive.

VII

The bishop had a limo on his drive.
He needed it to get to church to shrive
The punters who would manage to survive
His boring sermons and to meekly thrive
Through all the woes of his episcopate.
He'd give it to them straight, "Just don't be late,
My sermons are the greatest, they won't wait
While you expatiate upon the state

Of nations and dilate upon the weight
Of carrots to the pound or simply prate
About the sorry strait we're in, debate
The interest rate, articulate the fate
Of bishops." Are they dinosaurs or what?
We'd never miss a bishop: top the lot.

VIII

That limo sitting on the bishop's drive.
He needed it to get to church to save
His soul, empty the poor box in the nave,
Drive out the overnighting tramps then shrive
Them for their opportunist minds and strive
To make the wicked parish tarts behave
More meretriciously. The more he gave
The less decorum, should they hope to thrive.

And on his way out to the church one day
For his parishioners' largesse to pray,
He caught me twenty-five feet up a ladder
A martins' nest cemented to the gutter.
"You know," he said,
"What makes me so much sadder?
Your arrant cruelty, complete and utter."

IX

The bishop was disgruntled and annoyed,
So hurt to think that I could be so blind
To suffering endured within the mind
Of animals. A horse-whip he employed,
To give the kind of beating he enjoyed,
The very longest horse-whip he could find,
Designed to hurt like hell, to leave behind
So full of weals and confidence destroyed.

He said it hurt him so much more than me
But cruelty he could not tolerate.
Quails' eggs he had that afternoon for tea.
Kindness to animals could not frustrate
His noble plans that night when they would dish up
The very finest roast swan à la bishop.

X

The bishop was a man of many parts,
Well read, immersed in eschatology
And versed in biblical apology.
He captured all his congregations' hearts,
So kind was he to brassy local tarts,
A private lesson in biology
Would always trump epistemology
To profit from the knowledge it imparts.

Brocaded cassocks he would always wear,
Immaculate in his designer gear,
With mitre, spotless alb, and crozier.
"Clean living" made his life much rosier.
No filthy rake, he had long shafted hoes
And bedded pansies, Violet and Rose.

The Souks of Marrakech

A mere stone's throw from Spanish soil and what
A different world! In Marrakech the souks
Are dark and labyrinthine, full of nooks,
Crannies, twisted alleys: a lot you'll spot
Of lustrous fabrics, tapestries in shot
Silk, mint tea, carpets, maps and tourist books,
Curved Berber daggers and tagines (three cooks
It looks as if it took to lift one pot!)

Rock crystal, amethyst and peridot
And lapis, brazen coffee pots. Some grot:
Carved trinket boxes, olive, thuya wood.
Preferring to avoid the crowds you could
Steer clear of Atlas and of mountaineer:
The desert just goes on and on from here.

The Sea Snake

This reptile will excite remarks ungenerous
Because it can't survive the freezing deep.
Despite its being highly venomous
In warm littoral waters will it creep.
Unfortunately it is hated by
All tourists swimming on the Indic coast.
From Malabar to populous Mumbai
Hydrophidae left in the sun would roast.

Nor even Eve could be beguiled because,
Amphibious they're not, in fact or myth,
Repulsive more than Milton's serpent was,
No burnished sheen could it entice her with.
This creeping wretch, in thrall since time began
Its crawl might have forestalled the Fall of Man.

Though nearly Midsummer

Though nearly midsummer it is so why,
Deep in the forest, is there no bird song?
The shadows linger longer here among
The leaves, no gold or copper to defy
The fulsome green dye seen like stained glass high
Above. Where is the goldcrest? Where the throng
Of crossbills? Where the morning haze and long
Bright days ablaze with light and summer sky?

In all this cloying verdure nature's pledge
Of fruitfulness next year; in every flower
That falls the bud of next year's growth; in sedge
And pondweed shrivelled at the water's edge
New life; in every bower the latent power
Of life renews with light, sunshine and shower.

Uruguay

He flew to Uruguay and none knew why,
It never figured on his bucket list.
He didn't go on any sudden twist
Of fate. His hopeless purpose was to fly
Away somewhere and not return and try
To think none cared should he cease to exist.
It is a great achievement to be missed,
To have someone lament us when we die.

They fail in life that leave no mark, none there
To miss our being, nobody to care.
And Montevideo was there before
Him like that English 'phone box on the shore
At Maldonado just a bus-trip on,
And both will still be there when I am gone.

Knuckledusters in Montevideo

A pugilistic country, Uruguay.
In Montevideo I do recall
An open market: sold on every stall
Were knuckledusters, so surreal, but why?
Their minatory rôle would justify
A manufacturer's recall for all
Or 'phone call to the watchdogs to install
A Montevideo-recording spy.

And some of them were made of nickel-brass
And others steel and set with broken glass
Or garlanded with spikes and razor wire.
And to acquire one buyers don't require
A special permit, so for now don't try
To start a bar-room brawl in Uruguay.

Bored in Montevideo

Though Buenos Aires lies upon the south
Side of the sandbanks of the River Plate
And Montevideo lies at the mouth
And to the north, a map will demonstrate
To anyone who doesn't think it's true,
This useless piece of esoterica:
That Montevideo is closer to
The southern tip of South America.

It's further south than Buenos Aires' coast.
Of all our capitals third southernmost,
Of any city on this teeming earth,
The biggest boast of Uruguay and yet
In Montevideo there's nothing worth
A visit and there's nothing to forget.

The Shetland Isles

So bleak they are, so cold, the Shetland Isles.
We see the biting wind in every face
And no-one laughs with you and no-one smiles
In this forlorn and God-forsaken place.
In duffel coat and balaclava, scarf
And waterproofs, heads down, umbrellas sprout
From nowhere, from the neck down to the calf
We see transparent plastic macs, pulled out

Of rucksacks as the rain sets in again.
Commercial Street, its stones are greasy, wet,
And cold enough it is to freeze the brain,
And even when it's dry we can't forget
The drenching rain may not be here today.
Depend on it, it's always on its way.

5 A Penny for Them

The Intrinsically Impossible

So fortunate the few, those who insist
They've had such blessèd times from babyhood
They'd live them all again. Though they were good
Success not guaranteed, who could resist
A second stab at lofty targets missed?
With déjà vu and with hindsight we could
Deflect the storm and harness fire and flood,
Bring joy to all, our earthly woes dismissed.

We cannot live in retrospect. Desist
From thinking thus, for if we could we would
Abort our forebears; nip them in the bud.
Then nor could I nor humankind exist.
Absurd it is, we cannot ride roughshod
And heedless over reason, even God.

Ontological Speculation

To be or not to be that, without question
The substance of much ontologic egestion,
Gave Hamlet his bouts of congestion,
Trapped wind and severe indigestion.
When Osric let fly an improper suggestion,
He answered with "Out of the question!"

To be or not to be that is the query:
According to one old philosopher's theory
His thisness he called his haecceity,
His whatness encompassed his quiddity,
But only Duns Scotus's quoddity
Made Scotus an out-and-out oddity.

This soupçon of wisdom I hereby impart:
"I cogitate, therefore I am," said Descartes.
"Such learnèd profundities set me apart
From dimwits and dipsticks
who think they are smart."
One fat-head, though, deemed
that he must be because
He dreamed and he thought so and
therefore he was.

Malice Aforethought

Intentions count for all in casting blame
For wrongful acts: for righteous works acclaim.
It's how we must judge all deliberate deeds,
By purpose, not by how far each succeeds;
By all that we with knowledge of the facts
Foresee, the likely outcome of our acts
To be, but not by end results should they
Confound our expectations on the day.

Accountability

For those who try to plead that they were slewed,
To justify their rank ineptitude,
Inebrious or bibulous or stewed
To quell the victims of their turpitude,
Then I say drown them in the deep blue sea
Or bang them up and throw away the key,
For drunkenness should never be a way
To let our wicked thoughts lead us astray.

Empiricism and the Isle of Man

No man is an island according to Donne,
Philosophy lacking, his words were homespun.
But he was no Manxman or he would have seen
This Man *is* an island, it's sandwiched between
The Galloway coast and the shores of Antrim,
To get there you'll need to be able to swim.

That's why it's an island, John Donne is a clown,
He'll never climb down, we're just met with a frown.
Metaphysically speaking he'd argue away
That no-one can know and nobody can say
If Man is an island unless they have gone
All round it full circle according to Donne,

Or climbed to the summit of lowly Snaefell
To pirouette round its compact citadel
Finding sea from the start, coming back to the sea
All round them salt water, where else could they be?
No man is an island according to Donne,
But Donne didn't have his new spectacles on.

Platitudes

In others' grief, full of solicitude
Because we often feel inadequate,
We seize upon the nearest platitude
That we are able to articulate.
And even with the flash of insight sparks
Of wit are bromides, scarcely Attic salt.
They matter not a jot, our slight remarks,
If we can keep them honest to a fault.

While truisms are sadly much maligned,
Banal and humdrum you will often find,
Relayed by sycophant and parasite
They may be hackneyed and they may be trite.
Though overused and much abused pursue
The platitude for sometimes they are true.

Delusions on a Manchester Tram

While on a tram last Saturday a man
Gave up his seat for me. Though in a huff
Through sleeping rough my thanks polite enough,
To "Stuff it!" till his patronage began
To fan such rage as chronic dandruff can.
Four-letter words conveyed my gruff rebuff,
BO, bad breath and bedbugs big and bluff
Helped spread my fleas to this my latest fan.

I wonder did he envy me my age
And standing worship me as saint and sage?
He saw, perhaps with awe, what others saw:
A slab of alabaster without flaw
Transformed with stoic rigour over time
To this heroic figure in his prime.

To Excel in Self-Pity

I wonder if self-pity is the ache
Of all the worst, because it always throws
A pall of grief on *others* as it grows?
To be the victim, take the blame, forsake
Our kind like scapegoats, we must try to make
Our wasted lives heard loud above all those
Whose lives are just pathetic, make our woes
The object of our every hour awake.

To silence competition first we need
The loudest voice of all, the greatest grief,
The most exquisite pain beyond belief,
And only then will anyone concede:
Their own affliction's still the very worst
With which a human soul was ever cursed.

Police Brutality

There really is nothing that can excuse
Those children who employ brutality
Against our police force and hurl abuse
At every single officer they see.

Brutality against our noble force
Must not be turned by kind words or by gifts,
By lollipops and teddy bears of course,
As seldom charitable thought uplifts.

"Police brutality" trips off the tongue,
Reports of air rifles and half-bricks, vague
Sometimes, they may involve the very young.
Policemen must avoid them like the plague,

Or deal with their brutality in kind.
Socratic catechetics they eschew
For barbaric thumb-screws so well designed
They shorten almost any interview.

Interrogation means are rather brash,
For bastinado is a first resort;
The rack, the iron maiden and the lash
Reveal some "accidental" scars in court,

From coccyges impacted with steel bars,
Impressions made by battle-axe and truncheon,
From cigarette burns, hosepipe weals and scars
From stick and cudgel, cattle prod and bludgeon,

From broken bones in accidental falls
Down station stairwells, steps into the cells,
Against their young offenders' prison walls,
Their lively treatment finds no parallels.

It must be fairly plain to all of course,
The evidence will strongly indicate,
Children's brutality against our force
We simply will no longer tolerate.

Undoing What's Been Done

Undo what's done? It's patently absurd,
I'm sure semantists would agree with me.
What has been done *is* done and cannot be
Undone, unless the meaning of the word
Has blurred or yet another been conferred.
It cannot *not* have been done when we see
It clearly was done, though it may well be
You *could* redo what's done if you preferred.

So much of what we've done we *could* forget,
Delete, erase it from our minds as though
It never was, no-one may ever know,
But worse than this and far worse even yet,
Not doing what we should have done
When time for it has long since come and gone.

Guilt

Hereafter we persist though we are bare
Of outward guise, intangibly somehow.
The mind alone, guilt-ridden, can allow
Our conscience fear, our reason to beware,
As Judas might, to dread the night, despair
Of our redemption. As we disavow
Him here so thrice did Peter, but for now
Gethsemane may keep us unaware.

"The mind has mountains," Hopkins wrote; mistakes
Our headlong falls, and Adam's was the first,
The one that we were cursed with and the worst.
Their import is what guilty recall makes
Them as each shameful little deed contrives
To haunt us in our shameful little lives!

The Enigma of the Sphinx

Incomprehensibility, the key
To men's misunderstanding womankind.
Assigned a mind much kinder, more refined,
But having in tremendous quantity
Dissimulation and opacity,
It hardly tenders any peace of mind
For one inclined to find he's left behind
All but his lumpen transpicuity.

Now women-dacious inveracity
Is very different to men-dacity
For she pursues with assiduity
The ultimate in ambiguity,
Her thinking just as problematical
As any Sphinx is enigmatical.

Dystopia

Should we abide our misery in vain,
This dying progress from our birth, or bend
Its destined course? Fool's errand to contend
With nature's instincts. Give us all free rein.
Gratuitous constraints cause only pain.
We didn't ask to mend our ways or spend
Our days performing godly deeds. Why fend
Off evil thoughts and why should we refrain

From back-biting with all our innate spite?
It's natural to fight our comrades, smite
The feeble, blight the lives of others, slight
Our friends, kowtow to foes with all our might.
Why pity our good neighbour's sorry plight
When some of us are damned to darkest night?

The Passing of Our Days.

In salad days not grown enough to make
Us fearful for the coming of the night,
The sempiternal loss of light, the blight
Of everlasting sorrowing; to wake
Our dread of death, to make us ache and quake
In terror at the prospect of the sight
Of One who gave to us our blessèd light
And sent His Son to perish for our sake.

Then in the twilight of our years resigned
Are we to dread our mortal end, consigned
To chronic pain, tormented with ill-health,
Afflicted with shedloads of surplus wealth,
But then our imminent demise may find
That prayer will sharply concentrate the mind.

Regrets and Repercussions

Inconsequential are the things we do
Sometimes or things we don't, we don't know why.
So will we wonder far too late and sigh
To think that if we knew we could undo
The past before it starts, begin anew,
How many of us would instead deny
The imminence of fate to justify
Inaction in the face of all we knew?

So often small mistakes may have such long
Far-reaching repercussions that amaze
In hindsight. If we knew where we went wrong
Before we did so, might we change our ways?
If only we were able to return
To where we were, but would we ever learn?

Guilty Thoughts

I

Through idle thought alone if no-one knows,
We cannot hurt someone who never will
Find out. No victim: none could ever spill
The beans. Can we do any harm to those
Among our foes we would not if we chose?
Then who so harsh to charge us? Who would fill
Our hearts with guilt for actions that we still
Would not commit against those we oppose?

And is it not unfair to all of us
To think an evil thing is to have thus
Already in our hearts the evil wrought
Though it be no more than a passing thought?
If dire the deed, do we deserve damnation
Though we have laudably defied temptation?

II

How *do* we intercept our evil dreams
Before those evil dreams become a sin?
Our enemies, how can we simply grin
And bear the flood of calumny that seems
Designed to drown us in great turgid streams
Of rank abuse, to take blows on the chin,
To bear the insults and the fearful din
Of hatred issued forth in loudest screams?

How should we treat our earnest foes, to bring
The olive branch of peace, nor yet condemn
Them, turn the other cheek? No easy thing,
The hardest task of all to pray for them.
We all know what we really ought to do.
Will He forgive an errant thought or two?

III

Partaking in our frail humanity
We know His counsel of perfection sought
And found and followed is just as it ought
To be, Whose ideal world we'd all agree
Contains no fear and no disharmony.
But weakness manifested in a thought?
Our place in Paradise is dearly bought
If we must ever be as mild as He

In thought and action. And yet even Christ
Would drive the traders from His Father's house,
To money-lenders, vendors sacrificed.
Love for His Father showed no timid mouse
Was Christ for He was vexed and next would show
God's love above in blows bestowed below.

No Going Back

We feel our lives are slowly closing round
Us when the nights grow longer than the days,
When winter brings us sadness and malaise,
And all around us is a chill profound.
Across the moss the hare limps and the hound,
No heart to follow, with his master stays,
And grazing the horizon all the rays
Of Phoebus cannot gild the sallow ground.

It only comes with wisdom and with age,
The failings of our wasted lives engage
Our thoughts, so full of longings that we might
Have done things differently with second sight.
A different tack we'd take, another track.
Too late we find there is no going back.

Knowing When We are Blest

The trick it seems to me it is to know
Beyond a shadow of a doubt when we
Are really truly blest as we can be
And absolutely certain we are so.
To know at any moment we can show
That we are cheerful, revel in a sea
Of bliss, not being barely briefly free
From sorrow, for an instant clear of woe.

To be aware our feelings at the time
Could not be merrier: if we could climb
Out of the Slough of Despond and could shout,
With lungfuls of God's clean fresh air breathed out,
That "It is I, and joyful, you can see,
If I could fly no happier would I be."

The Nature
of Knowledge Today

I

The nature of our knowledge must have changed
Since we were at college or grammar school.
So many subjects are no longer cool
With Cicero and Tacitus exchanged
For TV stars, ephemera. Estranged
Are we from Virgil, Caesar, Ovid. Who'll
Read Latin grammar but a sorry fool?
Who'd study Greek apart from one deranged?

Though Batman, Donald Duck we might critique
What sort of freak can speak in ancient Greek
Apart from Homer (Simpson) whose boutique
Name reeks of the antique? But for the geek
The future of dead languages is bleak:
To study Plato simply isn't chic.

II

We don't expect young adults now to know
The things that once upon a time they would
Have been taught in their schooldays,
                things that should
Have been drummed into their heads long ago.
We don't expect our children now to glow,
With academic knowledge in their blood,
Where talk of "music" as now understood
Is not the violin or piccolo,

The French horn, trumpet or the clarinet,
The opera or oratorio,
The chamber orchestra or string quartet,
But merely youths who "sing" fortissimo,
Trite lyrics and the same old ditties drowned
By blasting tuneless electronic sound.

III

Ask any youth, he'll probably agree,
His expertise on anything to do
With football truly is immense, and few
The facts he doesn't know. Amazed you'd be
And staggered at the geography that he
Commands, from football teams in Timbuktu,
To every stadium in Kathmandu,
But nothing of the geography that we

Were taught at school, the geography he ought
To know, the knowledge you and I were brought
Up with. In history he'll never know
A single thing that happened long ago:
"Before my time," says he, "Before my birth
Was nothing worth recording on this earth."

IV

All past events are now of no concern,
Our antecedents are long dead and gone
And who would want them to live on and on?
Why ever should a schoolboy yearn to learn
About the past, why Alfred was to burn
The cakes, why Boadicea was the one
To spurn the Romans, how trench warfare won
The French the Battle of Verdun, to turn

The course of human history
With that enormous hard-won victory.
How costly was Gallipoli, how fraught
The war the ANZACs and the British fought.
And ought we to recall the debt we owe
Them giving us their all so long ago?

V

Possessing calculators we are freed
From needing to know how to multiply,
To subtract figures or divide them by
Each other. Numeracy we don't need,
And nor do we need books. We cannot read.
Our medium is television. Why?
Because it takes no effort to apply
Glazed eyes to screen, no effort guaranteed.

And do we really need to know the speed
Light travels in a vacuum to exceed
The speed of lightning, how enlightening
To know why we should find it frightening?
Discover why our fears are justified,
And why they shouldn't just be brushed aside?

VI

No longer do we need the human brain,
And no more need we know exactly why
The lowest common multiple of pi
Divided by its square root will obtain
The integer, the cosine and the plane,
The vector, congruent and radii.
No longer need we huff and puff and sigh:
Such facts indeed we don't need to explain.

As long as we know Galatasaray
Is still the capital of Turkey, why
The Capitol of Rome is Lazio.
Das Kapital of Marx we'll never know
Till Berlin fields a team to cap it all
Or Bayern Munich lets them have the ball.

6 Animals & Pathos

On a Boat to Barra

We sometimes do recall the oddest things.
Ten years ago and crystal clear the day,
A dog with me, we sailed from Eriskay
Aboard a boat and Barra bound. It brings
To mind the rain, the wind still sings and stings
And tears in gusts across the sound the way
It would, while gulls keep pace above the spray
On imperturbable and static wings.

Such moments unregarded in his prime,
They seemed inconsequential at the time.
The dog, so proud to be alive and when
He was he lived the here and now, but then
He questioned not the continuity
Of life, the permanence of him and me.

The Thoughts of a Dog

What really does go on inside the mind
Of the domestic dog? To simply say
They think of very little else all day
But eating what they're given, what they find
To feed on, would be callous and unkind.
Unique among all species is the way
They stay *by choice* with us: a dog's life they
Would say is so much better with mankind.

It isn't merely cupboard love that leads
Their kind to ours. They'd hunger if we halved
Their rations, linger with us if they starved.
Devotion trumps their nature and their needs,
As faithful Argos waiting twenty years
Rewarded only with Odysseus' tears.

The Plight of Animals

The plight of animals, how must it be
Ordained thus, either by a just God or
A merciful? By nature meek and poor,
They have no hopes, no future can they see
And all they own their living now as we.
No retrospect, their past is nevermore,
Their present short, a wretched end in store
Though dear their lives to them as mine to me.

Our ends will come in torment or at peace,
For we too hold mere tenure of a lease,
Yet for ourselves alone we fabricate
Futurity if we can expiate
The past. But why are helpless beasts outcast,
And who will give the sinless peace at last?

On a Farm in Westmorland

When very young we took a cottage here,
Long gone now with the farm, the barn, the stores
For forage, but we still recall the daws
That nested in its chimneys every year.
Adjacent in a field just to the rear
A tethered beast alone, we didn't pause
To question why, we hadn't any cause
To think its loneliness a little queer.

And we made friends with it and every day
We'd find the lushest grass and hay and strew
It round and talk the cattle-talk it knew.
And then it went on holiday, away
Inside a butcher's van. We wondered why
It went one day and didn't say goodbye.

Cruelty Born of Indifference

A documentary I long recall
About some primordial Papuan race,
A journalist looked very out of place
Where brutal savagery could befall
An animal so casually, for all
Were so inured, and such sights commonplace.
Impassive looks on each insensate face
That saw, trussed up and helpless in a sprawl,

Some chickens roasting whole upon the fire.
One still alive had sprung out of its pyre,
Its wings alight; its feathers had begun
To char. A tribesman took it by one foot
And patiently he turned and smiled and put
It back into the fire till it was done.

By the Temple of Luxor

The finest archaeology displayed,
We sat in silent awe above the Nile
And marvelled at each pylon, peristyle
And hypostyle and every colonnade
And obelisk and statue we surveyed.
But in the city by this noble pile
A wretched sight, the pathos of its vile
Neglect a single upright ear conveyed.

Upon a mule-drawn cart a mule just killed,
Its final gaze its stablemate's recoil.
A life drained with a knife, grey bowels spilled
Upon great sores born of relentless toil,
The ear they left still pricked upon its head
Could hear no more, should one revile the dead.

Fridtjof Nansen

It must be vainglory that prompts such aims.
In foiled attempts to reach the northern pole
He brought sled dogs with him, he gave them names.
As each grew weak and failed to serve its rôle,
Devised perhaps before his trip began
This famed humanitarian's intent,
Logistic and expedient his plan
To feed each to the others as he went.

And one by one he killed his dogs, a dearth
Of bullets made him slit their throats; the strong
Would wait much longer, having greater worth.
Their fate they surely knew for one among
The last and seeing that its ending neared
Took off across the ice and disappeared.

At the Boudhanath Stupa

So here we were at last in Kathmandu
To see among eight thousanders the heights
Of Everest, Cho Oyu, Makalu;
And down amid the seething mass the sights
Of this great dusty old metropolis,
Where round the Boudhanath Stupa we found
Stray dogs asleep: the warm sunshine was bliss,
Their simple need a little patch of ground.

But being *owned* is what they really crave.
One tailed us at a distance when we gave
It one kind word, discreetly tagged us for
Three hours till we returned to our coach door.
We climbed aboard and patiently it lay
Outside the door until we drove away.

A Little Incident
in North Wales

In memory and in dreams we don't know why
It is some scenes persist while others flee
The coming of the light. The Carneddau,
All else forgotten but for this: I see
Carnedd Llewelyn on a summer's day
In June, while tramping back in sultry heat
Along the Bangor road, the mournful way
He'd look down every grid between his feet

To view the water far below. His eye
Would turn to me as though somehow I might
Reward his wistful look: as well might I
Foretell how much had ended with that night.
His first mountain would be my last, would be
The first and last my dog would ever see.

A Razorbill's Egg, 1902

Upon a shelf it lies, a lifeless shell,
With Latin name misspelt in careful script.
Its emptiness belies the words that tell
Not of a life blown out or slowly dripped
From fragile refuge in its brittle shard;
Nor *why* a tender life was put away
Before the springtime of its birth. How hard
To say it never saw the living day.

Sule Skerry, reads the label, crags alive
As then with auks, and though in throngs they thrive
In raging seas and skies and soar and dive
In countless thousands, did it but survive,
The life inside that egg upon the shelf
Would still have been as precious to itself.

Pigs at the Fair

A summer country fair, no matter where,
And by the dodgems, swings and roundabout
In livestock pens found hereabouts are stout
Prize boars and bloated sows that cannot bear
Their weight but lie prostrate. Too late to spare
Them their impending fate, each comic snout
And corkscrew tail, each oink and squeak no doubt
Belies their desperation and despair.

And children here poke fun at them and mock
Their girth and make of them a laughing stock,
Or voice disgust, revile their fat and flab,
A preface to the shambles and the slab!
Their massive waistlines no-one could deny:
We fatten them to give us more to fry.

The Last Hours of a Piglet

Long-suffering are they. Should they complain
Who'd listen to their plaintive squeals, and who
Indeed would cater for their very few
And simple needs? These piglets cry in vain
For nourishment and comfort; inhumane
Their end, to die before they're weaned.
And through
The night they're starved before their hour is due,
It only adds discomfort to their pain.

And in a sty upon a concrete floor
They lie in stinking slurry mixed with straw.
Condemned to die for what we'll never cede,
The pressing need to feed our selfish greed.
Behind those frightened little eyes they know
For sure where they and all their brethren go.

Animal Suffering

A lifetime barely yields a pennyworth
Of joy for creatures innocent of mirth.
If this is bliss they share upon the earth,
Their happy days are numbered from their birth.
While we are guilt-encumbered with our kind
Sometimes we pity them, sometimes behind
Our rank and vain solicitude we find
We gain, not they, a little peace of mind.

Our hostile world He'll view awhile and smile
To mark the fertile margins of the Nile,
Where green shoots meet the waters to beguile
The antelope that feeds the crocodile.
Though scant the hope that seeds on meek despair
No sparrow falls, but He knows when and where.

The Mistle-Thrush

The mistle-thrush, there is no braver bird,
So keen in its defence of nest and young.
But during incubation rarely heard,
In silence broods, it lightly skulks among

The higher shoots and leaves. A hedge contrives
To hide its beating heart from thieving crow
That feeds upon the flesh of lesser lives
And struts around importantly below.

The courage of the weak unfledged rebels
Against the arrogance that arrogates
Defenceless foetal lives in fragile shells.
For in a brood of thrushes prey awaits:

No crows need feud for food, for foetus or
For brood to burgeon in the balmy hall
Of Chloris: fare aplenty, "hidden" store
Of squirrel and a free-for-all for all.

Survival of the fittest means no more
Than forte for the fattest to persist
In pinching from the poor as they ignore
All better thoughts, unable to resist.

All praise be to the homely mistle-thrush
Defending flimsy nest with care and zest
And ever watchful from that laurel bush,
Its heart loud-beating in its fearful chest.

Geese on the Moor

On Laddow Moss the April air is cold
And still. A single pair of wayward geese
We find beside a tarn, their nest of fleece
And feather sprigs of springy heather hold
Together. Once we found marsh marigold
Up here but now its meagre straggles cease
Their struggles to increase, stave off decease.
Too cold to let bog asphodel unfold.

The calm and peacefulness at night avails
Us in communion with the earth that fails
Us in the gales of March: listen, give ear:
The constant heartbeat of the earth you'll hear.
Enwrapped in darkness, lost to human sight,
The geese keep lonely vigil through the night.

A Burial on the Moor

We buried him upon the moss, three feet
It was below the level of the bog,
No need had he for linen winding sheet
Nor woollen shroud to fight the freezing fog.

Forlorn are they and cheerless, cold and bleak,
The moors. The wintry winds shriek down the cloughs
Unleashing constant driving rain. The reek
Of soaking peat pervades the barren groughs,

In places eight feet deep, and when it teems
The crumbling sheer walls of the haggs collapse
Into the grains or rivulets that feed the streams
And change their range and bearing on the maps.

Surviving rain and hail and sleet and snow,
The bog is always deeper where we know
The sphagnum moss and other mosses grow
And turn to peat, the moss of long ago.

The brown hare looks so foolish in its coat
Designed for winter wear, a cynosure
Upon the moss. So too sometimes the stoat
Bears snow-white fur that pads across the moor.

The cairn we built above his grave a guide
For twenty years the icy winds defied
Till one day it was scattered far and wide
Across the moor, across the mountainside.

We built another cairn a few months on
With flatter stones above his bones to pave
What lies below. The birds must know for none
Will ever sing or hop about his grave.

A place to sit and view the wilderness,
We could be anywhere, though close to this
Great teeming wen seen to the west, far less
A city, more a megalopolis.

The humus tang on brumous days would drown
The scent of heather on the moors and still
The sphagnum moss, the tawny, umber-brown
And bitter taste of acid peat would fill

The gales that drive the rain to Manchester,
That drain the sopping cloughs upon the moor.
The fog might linger week on week but there
The dog, a Labrador, would never more

Be seen upon the moor. He loved mankind.
He loved the moss, he loved the running free,
The vast horizons, being unconfined,
And he with me as he was born to be

Up on the open moor. He loved mankind.
We took him on the moss, left him behind,
We drowned his body on the sodden moor.
We left his body cold upon the moor.

And brave was he, but then all dogs are brave.
A dog, he wouldn't know what else to be.
His bravery died with him and his grave
Knows nothing of his trust and loyalty.

And all those years ago his weight was borne
Aloft and buried on the open moor.
His grave is deep and lonely and forlorn:
From breath of life his broken bones secure.

And forty-three years has he lain there hushed,
High on the moss, preserved by acid rain.
And ramblers will come and go, some flushed
With effort, some with pride, and some again

Will linger long but who knows what lies here
Below the tussocks and the quaking earth?
Enshrouded in the icy haze, nowhere
For living life, nor earth for giving birth.

Halcyon days are rare upon the moor,
When breezes waft the fragrant scent of ling
Across the moss. We startle grouse before
Us and they clatter off on noisy wing.

Move on in time: do you suppose they chose
To lie here twitching, blasted from the sky?
How Gloriously the Twelfth must baffle those
That did no harm and never hurt a fly.

Bilberry grows along with cotton grass
Upon the plateau's edge, widespread and dense,
And on the gritstone flanks the fleecy mass
Aflutter, found on every fold and fence.

The moor is silent now and dark and drear,
And seldom will we hear the blackbird sing.
The curlew rarely pipes from pastures here,
Nor skylark thrills with trills upon the wing.

The ouzel scarce on lofty gritstone edge,
The kestrels nest no longer on their ledge,
No whitethroat singing blithely from the sedge
Nor dunnock skulking in its laurel hedge.

And on the moor he lies, so cold is he,
Three feet beneath a weight of sodden ground.
No meadows filled with nature's harmony
Nor joyous concord of delightful sound.

Held fast upon the lonely moor he might
Have said, "Why leave me here? The night descends.
Your enemies I would have put to flight
But now may God protect me from my friends."

A dog that loved and was betrayed at last
By humankind. He thought we'd never part,
The status quo immutable, the past
Was past, the future present from the start.

For he lived in the here and now with me
And nor could I, by nature or design,
Live on in any other's memory
As his has been immortalised in mine.

On Bleaklow Hill

On Bleaklow Hill the Pennine Way that day
Lay featureless, all blanket bog and mist,
The kind of mist that will for weeks persist
To swell the humus scent of black decay.
Uncertainly the so-called Wain Stones, grey
And lichenous, loom livid in our midst,
Where to the vivid mind two boulders kissed,
The rest maintain recumbent disarray.

Beside the Kissing Stones, so sleek and braw,
A kestrel, murderous in beak and claw,
Equipped to grip and rip its prey apart,
A redstart plucked, stripped of its dripping heart:
No fear of us nor qualms of prissiness,
This falcon, plain to see, meant business.

A Skylark on the Moors

Sometimes the moors can beckon us outdoors,
Ablaze with light and bright with purple ling.
Because few songbirds sing upon the wing
That tiny speck above us gives us cause
To listen to the skylark as it pours
From tiny lungs its music in the spring,
Nor wrung from listless instinct does it sing
Of joyful days of freedom on the moors.

Cerulean blue the sky, no swallowtails
But cabbage whites, red admirals, long trails
Of mares' tails high above us give the lie
To promised rain, the peat moss tinder-dry.
But like the morning haze, the skylark's song,
Our summer days will never last for long.

The Dodo of Mauritius

This island nation scarcely can be proud
Of avifauna lacking common sense,
Surviving only in the perfect tense,
Their right to life, existence disavowed.
With beaks immense, these pigeons well endowed,
Why did they never peck in self-defence?
Their dovelike mildness giving no offence
They had no fear of man nor were they cowed

By hanger, broadsword, musket ball or pike.
As Eden was before the fall, childlike
Their innocence. Disarming was their trust
In humankind whose all-consuming lust
Could never cease its slaughterous bloodshed
Till every dodo in the world was dead.

The Old Man of Hoy

So sad it is and far away to think
Of where it led, the weaving track we'd tread,
The "we" the dog and me, the day we fled
From city life and almost in a blink,
It seems, we'd reach Great Britain's very brink.
The haunt of screaming kittiwake, we sped
On closely bitten turf, the track would thread
And zigzag through the bracken and sea pink

From Rackwick to the stack. If I could say
For certain then that bright and happy day
Could not return, how precious would it be?
If I could have the dog once more and see
Them flapping in the wind, those great big ears,
Would I give all my few remaining years.

The Oölogist

His eggs lie in their bird's-eye maple drawers;
With mapping pen and Chinese ink inscribed,
His records falsified, officials bribed.
Trephined with microtome and keyhole saws,
His eggs were blown with fine pipettes, sheer gauze
Infused with ethanol, details transcribed
In lusty learned tomes, such works imbibed
By ornithologists and crashing bores.

Its shell could not preserve the living bird
So why preserve with ink in written word
Its genus, species, race and common name?
To immortality it has no claim:
No seas of ink nor time spent in display
Could recreate the lives he took away.

7 Animals
&
Humour

Ode to a Labrador Retriever

The Labrador retriever
Is a very staunch believer
In a firmly held assumption
And sincerely felt presumption
That its humungous consumption
Of all inedible digestibles,
And indigestible comestibles,
Is indisputably irrefutably
Both delicious and nutritious
And well suited to a Labrador.

The Labrador retriever
Therefore, heretofore a carnivore,
Is furthermore an omnivore.
But the Labrador retriever,
In all diets non-believer,
Is unfortunately not unknown
To be singularly not unprone
To raging pantophagic fever.
To assist recuperation
And resist debilitation
They must desist from degustation.
Then deprivation and prostration
Under permanent sedation
Lead the Labrador to terminal frustration.

The Labrador Retriever

The Labrador retriever is a dog
Who's ill-disposed to cogitation or
Omphalic contemplation either for
He finds such lucubration quite a slog.
But rather than engage in monologue
Or talk with you (for barking's such a bore)
He'd much prefer to meditate (and snore)
And ruminate (and slumber like a log).

Although if he had half a chance he'd eat
Eight times his weight in finest cuts of meat
Before he'd answer Hypnos' weary call,
Or yet would yield to Morpheus and fall
In dreams for visionary food that's off
When he could wake and well and truly scoff.

An Epic Verse

In the Manner of Rabelais's Gargantua
and Pantagruel, the Polyolbion of
Michael Drayton and the Odyssey of Homer;
with Acknowledgment
to Shakespeare, Dante, Milton, Tolstoy,
Cervantes, Goethe, Schiller, Chaucer, Boccaccio,
Petrarch, Seneca and Heraclitus;
while Owing Much to the Labours
of Aeschylus, Aristophanes, Aristotle, Plato,
Plotinus, Virgil, Socrates, Euripides, Plutarch;
to Cicero, Eratosthenes and Demosthenes;
to the Eumenides, Gorgons and the Graiae;
to the Whole Panoply of the Gods,
but most of all, perhaps,
to Mr Edmund Clerihew Bentley:

A dog in the manger
Is in little danger
Of letting his manger
Be seized by a stranger.

A
Pan-
Egyri-
C address-
Ed to the La-
Brador Retriever

The Labrador retriever,
Gastronomic high achiever,
Compared with any other mutt,
When it comes to filling up his gut,
(Just when his dinner's in the offing
Or there's something worth scoffing)
On every last criterion, to the latter,
Our retriever is Hyperion to a satyr.
To consumption, with his gumption,
Knows all things are in subsumption
To his gourmandising, manducating,
Finding where his dinner's waiting.
When it comes to eating non-stop,
He'd take some beating, full stop;
There's no more eager beaver
Than a Labrador retriever.

(My barrel-shaped verse
Is a little the worse
For this soup-
Çon added
On)
*

A Working Dog in Calais

And dedicated to Letty, a Labrador retriever who,
in her ci-devant rôle as Chief Sniffer-Out, terrorised
so many would-be immigrants languishing at Sangatte

I

Along came she,
Yclept Letty:
When so critically unexpected
The Channel Tunnel
Became a funnel
For the politically disaffected.

II

She would with joy
Her nose deploy,
Performing as directed.
She little knew
For some sad few
Their fates she had effected.

III

That in her way
She would betray
The ones she had selected,
A desperate few
Who'd broken through,
She caught with skills perfected.

IV

With squeaky toy
Did she annoy
All those that she suspected?
Were they all squeaky clean,
Though keen,
Would she be so respected?

V

And would some be
More pleased if she
Her scenting rôle neglected,
So it became
A guessing game,
Her talents redirected?

VI

They're sent away,
To their dismay
Detected, then rejected,
Faux visitants,
Fake immigrants
And dodgy bods suspected.

VII

Nine years on,
Her work is done
And no more trucks inspected,
No more souls
With UK goals
To her fine nose subjected.

VIII

Her duties ended,
She befriended
Us, and snappily connected;
This rosy life
Has far less strife
She happily reflected.

IX

A great respite
For those in plight
With Letty deselected,
Here they're dwelling,
Numbers swelling?
Borders unprotected?

X

But she's retired,
No more required,
Her lâbôûrs circumflected,
And no more time
To find a rhyme
That goes with disinfected.

The Virtues of the Labrador

The Labrador retriever
Is a model of obedience,
A paragon of patience
And if you would believe her,
Unparalleled self-confidence.

The Labrador retriever,
Epitome of sapience,
Has unexampled brilliance;
You simply can't deceive her
With that level of intelligence.

The Labrador retriever
Is a nonpareil of continence,
To suit our own convenience;
Nobody could achieve her
Firm and self-restrained resilience.

The Labrador retriever
Thinks it little consequence
When it comes to global dominance;
The only things that grieve her
Are starvation and esurience.

Ailuro-Cyno-Machia
Cat Versus Dog in Cat and Dog Verses

I

Your dog you must pardon
If he poos in your garden,
Since your mog endeavours
To poo in your neighbours'.

II

The sated Labrador's
More oxymoronic
Than euphonic
Characteristics
Of nuclear ballistics,
According to statistics.

This overfilled omnivore's
Such a rara avis
(So unlike the mavis)
A very rare bird.
If it's ever occurred
Then nobody's heard.

III

Labs may pick
Up ticks and lick
Things utterly perverse,
But seldom roll in cat sick:
Things could be so much worse.

IV

The Labrador tries
To meet our eyes,
The windows of our souls,
It's said.
The cat's content to greet
Our soles
And meet our feet
Instead.

V

Hapax Dogomenon:
A word used only once
For the nonce
Unless your retriever
Has recurrent parrot fever.

VI

Does a Labrador retriever
With a satellite receiver
Need to own a dog and bone
If he wants to 'phone home?

VII

An aged agnostic retriever
In doctrine is no great believer,
His dog-ma's his dam,
His dam is his mam,
(Not the dam that is built by a beaver).

VIII

The dog is resigned to being maligned
For pooing in public places.
The cat of your neighbour is far more refined,
Combined with its airs and graces,
Its behind is aligned with your garden in mind
Where it poos in its own private spaces.

IX

The dog doesn't hanker for squalor or need
To loudly proclaim its enslavement.
If freed from its owner, collar and lead
Your dog wouldn't poo on the pavement.

X

Would the Reverend Spooner
Say his hunting ground's dull bogs
A tad merrier, and sopping wetter?
With his whore bound, the hag drowned,
He drained her togs to dry them.
Would she that boggy ditch fill full
With other soggy bods?

Would the Reverend sooner
Spay his grunting hounds, bulldogs,
A mad terrier, and whopping setter?
With his boar hound, the drag hound,
He trained her dogs: do try them.
Should we that doggie bitch fulfil
With other boggy sods?

Verses Addressed
To Sundry Labrador Retrievers

I

Letty the Labrador lost her ball,
She didn't know where she had dropped it:
An appalling pratfall
Left me sprawled in the hall
From the top of the stairs where she'd plopped it.

II

Her training was sadly protracted
She was ever so sorely distracted
When she lost all her teeth
(It rhymes with beneath)
Her attention was grossly impacted.

III

She barkth with a runthible lithpth
Eatth nothing but runthible crithpth
Now she'th lotht all her teeth
(Thtill rhymth with beneath)
'Tith time she was thadly dithmithed.

IV

There was a fine canine called Ellie
Whose ears were as big as your telly
Those trips to the deli
For marrowbone jelly
Gave Ellie a very large belly.

V

When she stopped chasing cats off the lawns
We rescinded her ration of prawns;
But she got so forlorn
Depressed and withdrawn,
She expressed her distress with her yawns.

VI

There was a bright canine called Lucy
Who loved Schopenhauer and Debussy:
Converting Hispanics
To quantum mechanics
She rendered the works of Zanussi.

VII

A vigorous canine called Rover
Just loved rolling over and over,
He took off from Leeds
Reaching breakneck speeds,
(Cartwheeling moreover)
By Ealing in clover,
He made a stopover in Dover.

VIII

A precocious young canine called Vida
Was bought for a song from a breeder;
By two she was expert in matters abstruse,
At three she was reading the novels of Proust
And by four singing Franz Schubert's lieder.

IX

The Labrador to whom I alluded
Above with a Newfoundland sadly concluded,
Her "starvation ration"
Belied her great passion
And the twenty-six stones she obtruded.

X

There was a young canine called Letty
Who was partial to fish and spaghetti:
When you squeaked her old squeaker,
Her scran would she seek her,
To scoff with the charm of a yeti.

XI

Bold Lucy would get in a pique
And tell us the future looks bleak,
That toys can't be toys
If they don't make a noise
On account of their missing a squeak.

XII

Young Rover would get very cross
If his teeth one attempted to floss:
His dental aesthetician
Cum odontological prosthetician
Cum dietetical cosmetician,
Was naturally at a great loss.

XIII

A ponderous canine called Letty
Squashed three beds and a Chippendale settee:
Her weight was so great
That her mates would debate
If it equalled a ton of confetti.

XIV

Letty has a little trick
If you throw her a ball:
Because she is a little thick
She'll bring you back a little stick
Or someone else's ball at all.

XV

Lucy had a better trick
Should you fling her a stick:
She'd sometimes sling it back at you:
"I've not come out to play," she'd say,
"Your same old silly games today,
I've better things to do."

XVI

Letty's tail will wag all day,
It means she wants to play:
It also means
She's full of beans,
It may swing either way.

XVII

At agility jumping our Vida
Was doglegged and dogmatic leader,
Better known for her looks
And her poetry books,
For the garden she'd sown
With the bones that she'd grown,
Dogged weeder and doggerel reader.

XVIII

Rover was a wayward dog
Who used to swig eggnog:
It helped promote
His healthy coat
(From John Moore's catalogue.)

XIX

Ellie was our dearest hound,
Her kindness was unsought,
For all the gifts she found
For us and every prize she brought.

XX

Rover was the first of them,
A rough-cut little gem,
With talents unrevealed
We never knew what lay concealed;
Then Vida, avid anagram
And gentle as a lamb;
Ellie was the kindest soul;
Her passing left a hole
That Lucy filled, her mighty brain
A strain at first, a pain to train
But then revealed to yield the field
To none for trophy, cup and shield.
And last came Letty, she whose tail
In greeting never ceased to flail,
In eating more, in overeating even more
Than any other Labrador.

The Intractability of Cats

In fancy, truth, or vision, lies or worse,
With honesty or ingenuity,
Congruity or ambiguity
The mind can roam the globe, the universe,
Pluck stars from distant galaxies, traverse
The Andes, bring the world to unity,
Resolve community disunity
And conjure up the most atrocious verse.

But there are things that no man can achieve,
One cannot herd a cat of fertile age
Or make a cat of any age relieve
Itself within its privy curtilage.
Remember cats are all submersible,
Averse to doggerel verse and worsible.

Barney: A Cocker Spaniel

The worst thing I recall he ever did,
Before our very own mince pies he whips
A carrot from the fridge!!! With Freudian chips
And whopping nose he lies, "I thought I hid
Some plausible pork pies in there amid
The filchards, pickled tea leaves, purloined steaks,
The rustled sprouts, poached yeggs and stollen cakes,
The carrot simply flew away it did!!!"

In those few years he lived he charmed us all,
And never took another carrot though
We often wished he would. He'd deftly show
Obedience while keeping us in thrall:
Do *we* manipulate them, or do *they*
Manipulate us? Difficult to say.

Herding Cats

The cat you cannot herd, no dog can tend
Like sheep a cat unpenned, though cats defend
Their stance, contend their brains by far transcend
The herd they condescendingly offend.
Though hard to comprehend, you can't befriend,
Commend or vilipend your cat, depend
On it, they couldn't really care. Suspend
Them by the nether end I'd recommend.

Post-dogtoral research finds herding balks
The cat's developing a finer skill,
The need to creep up silently and kill.
No dog could herd a creeping wretch that stalks.
The feline wants no social life, and that's
Why dogs can neither herd nor muster cats.

The Thankless Toad

One sultry day in midsummer I found
A common toad as dry as dust and prone
Upon my half-baked drive, a cobble stone,
No respite and no shade upon the ground.
In searing heat it lay, made not a sound
For gutting toads alive are cats well known.
Here too the jackdaws and the crows have flown
Their sound the rat-a-tat of magpies drowned.

I took that toad and left it in the shade,
Looked back to see the difference I had made.
No thanks. Writ large upon its face was clear
Ingratitude, peeved attitude, a trace of fear
There too, but with that sneer on me bestowed,
The last kind deed I did for any toad.

A Black-Listed Species

The avian community is glad
He's dying out, the mad oölogist.
With every species on the British list
He always wanted more eggs than he had,
And on his checklist those he had to add
Were those his greedy eyes could not resist.
So sad, this would-be ornithologist,
So sad he was, and just a trifle mad.

In spring our conscientious eggers thieve
The eggs of godwit, pratincole and stilt
That nest on shoreline rocks with ruff and reeve,
On mudflats and littoral sand and silt.
They should be galvanised, the whole bang lot,
With fifty thousand gigawatts or shot.

The Trials of the Oölogist

Surmounting cliffs to squalid ravens' nest,
Or scaling sixty feet of beech to thieve
The eggs of rook and heron; (cuckoos *leave*
Their own in pipits' nests: but still a pest
To pipits, latest figures would suggest).
Subvert routine, you see, all birds will grieve.
To slay a latent being won't relieve
Its layer of the feeling dispossessed.

For you can see it in the eyes of those
That having lost their charges don't know where
To turn but hop from branch to branch, disclose
Their loss, disconsolation and despair.
Their bird brains cannot suffer mental pain?
Just open up your eyes and think again.

The Bandy Black-Backed Bustard

This bird, a rara avis on the moors,
Has two great bandy black-backed bustard's legs
Whose feet are reinforced with iron segs
But cannot match the buzzard's fearsome claws,
Its fell intent, or give it any pause
For thought, to question why the bustard's pegs
Are back to front or why its coiffure begs
Contrast for exiguity with yours.

The bandy black-backed bustard maybe might
Make of itself a most unpleasant sight
When all its beaky wattles are awobble
To imitate a turkey-cock agobble.
But happily its lot is not the pot
For taste, advisedly, it hasn't got.

The Egg-Collector and
His Worthy Contribution
to Obstetrics

His birds' eggs looked so chic in simple polished
frames,
All velvet lined they were, laid out to kindle flames
Of inexpressible excitement in the names

Of all the birds whose speckled eggs were on display
Therein; the taffrail, guttersnipe, and Parmese grey,
The pilcrow, spine-tailed swift and gaudy popinjay.

Behind its glass, he signed and dated and assigned
To each a dodgy provenance and disinclined
Was he to have his attributions undermined.

His egg-collecting proved to be a mere pretence,
A front. (Collecting empty shells made little sense
And should, he thought, be made a capital offence).

Gas chromatography would subsequently bare
Each egg for what it was despite his crafty care.
In spite of all his cunning subterfuge they were

All found to be identical. His faulty claim
Lay in his giving each a different common name;
Two hundred eggs they were and every one the same!

The so-called bandy black-backed
bustard's egg misled,
For this was thought at last to be a thoroughbred
Rhode Island red or leghorn, not the egg he said.

Besplodged with umber protoporphyrin they ain't,
Of sky-blue oöcyan they bore not a taint,
He simply daubed them with lots of acrylic paint.

This errant boffin's diligent experiments
On which he'd squandered most of his inheritance
Had led him inexorably to strange events.

He was at length unwittingly revealed to be
An arcane anatomical anomaly,
For every single egg he laid himself you see.

And by his own thankless travail he blazed a trail
That women could not fail to find of some avail:
With all the pains of childbirth he'd assail the male.

And he'd progressed as far as laying addled eggs
But his assiduous and avid research begs,
Or rather prompts, the guarded question,
"Laying eggs?

Is that a fit and proper job for men to do?
And what you might expect male cockatoos to do,
Male mews or hoopoes, tinamous or doos to do?"

To think of such a hare-brained scheme!
That stupid man!
But then it has been said he was far madder than
The maddest madman since the very world began.

Cyclostomous and lamprey-like his open gape,
They shut his mouth with twenty yards of parcel tape,
Hands tied behind his knobby knees to foil escape,

He had his eyelids seeled just like a sparrowhawk's,
Extended on the rack was he à la Guy Fawkes
When (lawks above!) he grew a pair of comely norks!

The all-male jury took three minutes to decide
He suffered from an overweening sense of pride
And was found guilty, he, of pantogenocide

In prospect, for the population of the earth
Would die out as mankind would think
it scarcely worth,
The tribulation and the grief of giving birth.

And he was promptly charged with
causing mass alarm
And frog-marched footly to the local funny farm
Where it was hoped that he could do
no further harm.

To think the way he did, that very stupid man!
But then he proved to be far greatly madder than
The maddest madman since the very world began.

8 Animals & Soul

I Well Remember

I well remember those poor sightless eyes
Still bright, that held reflected just what we
Could see, not he, detached from all that he
Had known. The lonely moors, the open skies,
The smell of heather, peat and rain, where rise
The grouse on clacking wing; no more to be
Among the boundless Pennine hills, nor see
Beyond our being what before him lies:

Another image bare, but far more bleak
I witness in those eyes and see it still.
We hold not for our beasts the hopes that will
From our conceit arise, yet who more meek
Than he should be among those creatures worth
The love of Christ, inheriting the earth?

Of All God's Living Creatures

Of all God's living creatures only we
With subtle artifice create our style
Of dress and image, and with painted smile
Construct the me we want the world to see.
Though what they are is all that they can be,
Would any beast consider it worthwhile,
Supposing he were able, to beguile
His kind with such conceit and vanity?

"I want no artful guise," says one, "I know
No other self but mine: I seldom speak,
Though proud am I, I have no need for show.
With each among my kind I am unique:
And never will, ordained before my birth,
My like be seen again upon this earth."

It Might Have Been
Just Yesterday

It might have been just yesterday, the leap
From earth to the abyss in which he lies;
Not sleeping in that chasm, for sleep implies
That he will wake again, that we might keep
A lamp lit in the dark. There is no sleep:
Let Eden be the vilest villain's prize,
For beasts only the blackest midnight skies
Await them and the coldness of the deep.

Untroubled he, his little life affirmed
His transient joy, with shadows unconcerned.
Before the light that thwarts serenity
And innocence and opened up our eyes,
Scant reason stayed his happy infancy
While wisdom merely makes me *worldly* wise.

Descartes and Animal Pain

Descartes tells us sensation marks mankind
From all the beasts, their feelings less than stone.
Because they suffer silently we find
They suffer not at all: it helps condone
The hunter if the hunted feel no pain.
The gutted wildebeest will mutely fall,
It seldom shrieks, in dying won't complain.
The end can't be so dreadful after all.

It cannot be, or wouldn't it be odd,
Those sparrows sold, two farthings paid for five,
Not one of them forgotten before God?
How could some great celestial joke contrive
Not only for a few of us to thrive,
We eat each other barely to survive?

One Night I Dreamt

One night I dreamt I saw a land where lies
A mountain peak remote and proud, ablaze
With arctic light from infinite displays
Of unfamiliar stars. I saw it rise
To vast untrodden heights while otherwise
Unseen, through cliffs of diamond ice, a maze
That led to left and right by hidden ways
But ever on and upward to the skies.

Then heard a voice: "They merit in their way
Far more than you, for innocents they are."
And saw them next to heaven from afar,
Numberless, full of happiness and play,
And romping in the snow quite unconcerned.
I called, and one among them stopped and turned.

We Don't Know
What They Are

We don't know what they are, nor why they're here,
We know not whence they came nor where they go,
But some of them give comfort to the low,
Some help the blind to see, the deaf to hear.
They leave us poignant memories that cheer
And some that ache, remembered deeds that show
The lowly creature kindnesses we know
Once Eden knew when Eden knew no fear.

We don't know what they are and never will,
But sure it is they know themselves and learn
And think and understand, when parting yearn
For us and grieve sometimes; and sometimes still
It feels we would be better, to my mind,
Allied with them and far less to our kind.

Aristotle, St Paul and Plato

We don't know what they are or what they know
But Aristotle would on each bestow
A soul to any able to decode
Wise logic from a foetal nematode.
St Paul insisted humans on the whole,
Possess a body, spirit and a soul.
The last two, though, he wasn't able to
Discretely view or separately pursue.

While Plato's Greek was stylish if obscure,
His Latin was so bad he wasn't sure
The soul in posse with the body was
So briefly with its anima because
The corpus doesn't last in esse long,
Or doesn't know in se what's right or wrong.

Aquinas and the Soul

Aquinas said the body with the soul
Make both sides of the pair a single whole,
The mortal and immortal are combined
As one part with the other intertwined.
But in this godless age we don't believe
In anything our eyes cannot perceive
As we pragmatic quack philosophists
Debunk dogmatic psychopannychists.

With future goals in view a faithful few
Do not believe we're finished when we're through.
The few who fondly feel their futile strife
On earth deserves a wondrous afterlife
May find their final fate as fiery as can be,
Though lasting only an eternity.

Custodians of the Earth

Custodians of the earth they sometimes call
Themselves, a view that's not hard to gainsay.
Compare our lives with theirs: compare the way
That we poor brutes have scarce the wherewithal
To toil, to bear our burdens, and to haul
In chains the plough or harrow meagre clay
So they can scorch the land while they inveigh
Against our indolence. For after all

This bounteous world is one great free-for-all
For all to fight for and for all to feel
(For they are godless too now, not in thrall)
It's their entitlement, they're free to steal
What's ours, expediently, from the weak,
The down-at-heel, the poorly and the meek.

A Winter in Uzbekistan

A winter in Uzbekistan so cold
And raw and brittle, on the steppes some years
Ago, the day we saw three dogs whose ears
Had crudely been cut off, so we were told,
To render them more docile, more controlled.
It kept their livestock safe, quelled farmers' fears;
An outrage to their nature it appears,
To maim those dogs to bar their being bold.

And then we noticed one of them had lost
A leg. His kennel-mate would lean daylong
Against him, keep him upright in the frost:
In such a manner both would get along.
Compassion surely taught one to assist,
As surely trust helped both to coexist.

What Walt Whitman Thought

Walt Whitman thought that he could turn and live
With animals, extolled their innocence,
Their inner peace and tolerance. They give
Their all to serve us, die in our defence;
As with the she-wolf in the Lupercal,
Who fed the infant founders of the state
Of Rome, their unsought kindness surely shall
Ensure there should a greater good await.

With no eternal soul there is no prize
For honest beasts that strive for us, their whole
Lives spent in servile toil they recognise
Our lordship and accept their humble rôle.
How hard it is to meet those patient eyes,
To mark their depths and say we see no soul.

The Hounds

The hounds were bound to frown:
their caves were found
By Homo troglodytes, who'd impound
Them and surrounding ground for miles around.
But our confounded homeless faithful hound
Was found to be so sound to have around,
In guarding property so well renowned,
Was bound at last profoundly to redound
With all resounding credit to the hound.

So it's a playground, not a battleground,
And far from downing them we've roundly crowned
Them, clowned with them and
let them hang around.
They keep us spellbound, cleverly dumbfound
Us, skills I would propound except I'm bound
To say I'm now too browned off to expound …

Perhaps this Earth

Perhaps this earth is all they'll ever know;
Denied the chance of immortality,
Denied the transport to serenity
Where we expect the righteous to go.
But hopes of what in grace He may bestow
On man they cannot apprehend as we;
And what they cannot think, believe or see
They cannot know and cannot thus forego.

We like to think with C S Lewis though,
That some of them with special insight may,
In sharing theirs with ours in some small way,
Enhance our lives beyond the grave to show
The better sides of our humanity,
Surviving not alone in memory.

Some Fifty Years have Passed

Some fifty years have passed now since the day
We found a white goat tethered to a stake
And left to starve atop the moor on Eriskay,
A lonely end, a cruel one, to make
This sacrifice with biblical assent
A scapegoat in the wilderness. So strange,
The perfect ring of naked earth that bent
Around the stake, the limit of its range.

Beyond its tether nothing but reproof,
The caprine lecher or the silly goose,
A parody of Pan with cloven hoof.
No need this Pan for Aristotle's nous:
Advised to chew the rope, with weary voice
The goat would claim it made the better choice.

Dominion is Ours

Dominion is ours without the key
To understanding them, the thoughts behind
Their eyes or what they know. We're loth to find
Brute faculties exceeding ours, to see
That while they have no comic repartee,
Lack logic, abstract thought or scheming mind,
They've other senses greatly more refined
Than ours and more intense in their degree.

How dare we say they lack our sentience,
Endorsing slaughter, while ostensibly,
It lets us treat them reprehensibly.
All beasts are subjects of a life, they sense
And feel, and still some claim they have no pain
Because they are too stoic to complain.

The Blackbird

So what can make this joyous songbird sing
That cannot but proclaim its blackbirdhood?
In fairest weather and in foul it could
Convey nought but the utmost joys of spring.
So fling right open all the doors, and fling
The windows wide: they don't feel, as they should,
The cold that blasts the dingle in the wood,
So let the blackbird sing of warmth and bring

New life as from the rhododendron bud.
The prospect of the spring now fills the wood
With songbirds' song and in such fluting voice
To celebrate creation and rejoice:
The blackbird sings with glee, for he knows he,
As he himself, no other self can be.

9 Poles & Penguins

À la Mode in Antarctica

The boffins in Antarctica are well
Adapted to the climate on the ice.
Among the most exclusive personnel,
For stylish kit they pay a tidy price.
To wow the penguins and to look their best
They wear top-flight designer gear. Forget
The rest, the long johns and the thermal vest,
Rucksack and anorak. The egg-head set

Profess finesse expressly to impress:
Pink top-hat, tails, skink shoes and lustrous mink
With aigrette feathers, ostrich plumes and dress
In cloth of gold. The penguins shrink to see
Such panoply, the penguin suit they think
To be the fashion statement's apogee.

The Problem with Penguins

So many penguins in Antarctica
Still seem to think they own the continent.
Because they brood for ages standing bent
They often get severe sciatica.
Their cousins live in South America,
And consequently they're incontinent.
To find out more consult the eminent
Encyclopedia Britannica.

Most of the penguins in Antarctica
Are very partial to eschscholtzia.
Alas, you see the plant (it's news to me)
Is only found in North America.
But should you ever need to spell it see
The Shorter Oxford English Diction'ry

Robert Falcon Scott

Was Scott a hero or a man to whom
Our histories have mostly been too kind?
Impossible to say or even find
His parallel today, where we presume
So much of others should a danger loom,
And mobile phones now bring us peace of mind
Where terra incognita once resigned
Us to the prospects of an icy tomb.

Remotely now, where satellites can pry,
We can be found and rescued unfulfilled,
Few true heroic exploits left to try,
Just as in wartime most of those now killed
Are shot, or gassed, or blasted *from afar*,
We've very few heroics left in war.

Spitsbergen

Six hundred miles to reach the pole from here.
And there's no crime because full well all know
Where each man lives. As one they come and go,
To dodge suspicion, keep them in the clear.
And here, it seems, you cannot volunteer
To croak. They cannot cope with corpses so
Prospective corpses are required to show
Respect, to pack their bags and disappear.

And this is not a place to be caught short.
In such a pristine land with so much snow
It's hard to know exactly where to go,
And much more dodgy than you might have thought.
Encounters with the polar bear are fraught
But you can shoot them as a last resort.

To Woo the Penguins

The penguins of Antarctica, we meet
Them nesting with their young. They find the ice
Conducive to the health of little feet.
Their next-door neighbours are not very nice.
They poke each other's eggs and young, and when
One looks away another one will thieve
The priceless pebbles from its nest and then
Evacuate its calling card and leave.

To woo the penguins and indulge their taste
Regurgitate Antarctic squid and krill;
Seduce them with the pukey putrid paste,
But give them jellied eels from Tower Hill
Upset the frail ecology, lament
The certain death of the environment.

Sphenisciformès

Antarctica is full of experts who
Work with Sphenisciformès every day
And yet they cannot understand the way
The penguin population would eschew
The continent if they were able to.
They find it isn't easy to convey
The reason they're so very loth to stay
While these experts their ologies pursue.

According to the humans on the ice,
The smell of penguins scarcely would entice.
They find it most unsatisfactory
To sensibilities olfactory
Yet strange to say, the penguins counterclaim,
The humans should be taking all the blame.

Not Reaching the North Pole

Bold Frederick Cook the very first to get
In pole position so the man maintained;
He drained the Arctic Ocean for, it pained
Him to relate, he didn't like to let
His feet get wet and hadn't learned yet
How to walk on water he explained.
(He didn't even part the waves, he gained
The pole by trawling through the internet.)

Then Peary's claim, a barrelful of laughs,
No-one believed his dodgy photographs.
In every snap he's taken at the pole we see
A horde of gibbons swinging tree to tree
In sunhats, shades, engaged in wanton romps
Aloft amid the torrid mangrove swamps.

Birds and Boffins

Antarctica, the final continent,
The only one unpeopled and unspoiled
By all bar billions of boffins bent
On working out how tourists may have soiled
The landscape with their toxic presence there.
Pre-empting all empirical research,
"These tourists," they dogmatically declare,
"Can't touch a blinking thing they don't besmirch."

Tourists, unlike the penguins, will insist
They damage neither fragile sea nor land:
"We don't scoff all that fish, we don't persist
In defecating in the snow or stand
There grumbling away while we pollute
The continent dressed in a penguin suit."

Bear Island

From iridescent veils above they flow,
Diaphanous festoons of light. We prize
The sight at night, cold fires in glaucous skies.
In daylight and the gannets come and go,
Mount Misery, Bear Island lies below.
Too bleak these freezing seas to colonise
All but abandoned land, forlorn it lies.
Abhor the loathsome flies, abhor the snow,

Abhor the hoary drifts, the icy clifts,
The slimy creeping things that haunt the deep.
Some sense at length brings wings to me, uplifts
Me whence my soul gives ear the while I sleep:
I fear you steer too near the siren choir:
To raging hate no loving hearts aspire.

10 Ninety (Mostly) Clerihews

Ninety (Mostly) Clerihews

I

George Frideric Handel
Was known as a terrible vandal
Until he chopped up his harpsichords
To make stylish new skirting-boards.

II

Thomas Hardy
Was rather foolhardy.
Drinking creosote with his Bacardi
He was rather more fool than hardy.

III

Mary Queen of Scots
Often had the trots,
But hacking off her head
Put her hacking cough to bed.

IV

Johann Sebastian Bach
Was admired for his fine antiquark.
Drinking coffee with his cantatas,
Prattling particle physics with his toccatas.

V

Edmund Clerihew Bentley
Was hardly up to it mentally.
Compared to McGonagall his verse,
At best could scarcely be worse.

VI

Edmund Spenser
Vented his spleen on his censor,
With language obscene he'd often been seen
With his epicene on-screen Faerie Queene.

VII

Archbishop Tutu
Kept in his mitre a hoopoe,
But few zulus knew the ensuing to-do
Was due to the cuckoo that flew up his tutu.

VIII

Francis Bacon
Was often mistaken
For Shakespeare.
How queer.

IX

Edward Lear
Would simply disappear
To avoid being taken
For Francis Bacon.

X

John Keats
Was known for his scholarly feats.
But on first looking into Chapman's Homer
"Translation" he thought a misnomer.

XI

Franz Joseph Haydn
Hoped he could widen
His repertory total
From garage to grunge to motets sacerdotal.

XII

Queen Boadicea
Was constantly prone to diarrhoea
But after her bout of glue ear
Nobody wanted to see 'er.

XIII

Isambard Kingdom Brunel
Was widely acclaimed for his Box tünnèlle
But his Clifton suspension bridge
Received less coverage.

XIV

Arcangelo Corelli,
With the mind of Machiavelli,
Was a great virtuoso with the concerto grosso,
But his counter-intelligence was only so-so.

XV

John Milton
Was fond of his Stilton,
Having his copy of Paradise Lost
All over embossed at very great cost
With the town and the cheese it was built on.

XVI

Sir Leslie Stephen
Found the Alps so uneven
He renamed the Matterhorn
The Should-Be-Much-Flatterhorn.

XVII

George Frideric Handel
Caused no little scandal
When the castrato sang his librettos
Wearing string vest and bile-green stilettos.

XVIII

Charlotte Bronte
Got the full monty
When the Chippendales briefly
Visited Keighley.

XIX

Charles Dickens's
Books are right thick 'uns,
And his Old Curiosity Shop
All Greek to Aesop.

XX

Salvador Dali
On a visit to Bali
Swore in Somali, swore more in Bengali
And twirled his moustache in Kigali.

XXI

Anthony Trollope
Deserves a great wallop.
His Barchester Towers
Goes on for hours.

XXII

Immanuel Kant
Knew his brain cells were scant
When he started the silly season
With his lightweight Critique of Pure Reason.

XXIII

Arthur Schopenhauer
Felt life had turned sour.
He got very cross when he failed to forestall
Doctor Pangloss from ending it all.

XXIV

Joseph Mallord William Turner
Once had a good earner,
Sadly unaware the Fighting Temeraire
Lay toasting on his back-burner.

XXV

Jonathan Swift
Set his hero adrift
And so
Did Daniel Defoe.

XXVI

Friedrich Nietzsche
Had only one interesting fietzsche.
Spelling the name of this crietzsche
Perplexed his philosophy tietzsche.

XXVII

Gottfried Wilhelm Leibniz
Was delighted to find that his fried bits
Rhymed nearly as neatly as a wheat-free bagel
With Georg Wilhelm Friedrich Hegel.

XXVIII

Christopher Marlowe
Plotted his way from Chigwell to Harlow.
In Deptford he blotted his copybook,
Got stabbed then adopted a floppy look.

XXIX

Ludwig van Beethoven:
After it was proven
He was Mutt and Jeff,
They wouldn't trust him with the treble clef.

XXX

Sir Christopher Wren,
The building market then
In jeopardy, thought it rather witty
To set fire to the City.

XXXI

Nicholas Hawksmoor
Like Wren and Guy Fawkes, more
Inclined to burn down without pity
Than daub with graffiti so pretty a city.

XXXII

Queen Victoria said "We are not amused"
When mildly accused of being confused,
"We are a queen and therefore excused being lax
With some aspects of pronominal syntax."

XXXIII

George Frideric Handel
Wouldn't hold a candle
To Brahms and Liszt,
Were he their consultant proctologist.

XXXIV

Poor Aeschylus is dead. It has been said
An eagle dropped a tortoise on his head.
Just think what he could have taught us
About probability theory and the tortoise.

XXXV

Queen Anne
The last of the Stuart clan:
She failed to produce any viable successors
Despite hints from hosts of reliable hairdressers.

XXXVI

Samuel Pepys used simple techniques
To keep his neat diary sheets for weeks
From sneak peeks. No need for a padlock to outwit
Paul Pry: just think of a code and forget it.

XXXVII

Empedocles
Thought it quite a droll wheeze
To leap into Etna's crater.
Still missing three thousand years later,
Beginning to invoke a sense of unease.

XXXVIII

Are De Koonings's doodles
Worth whole caboodles
Of Jackson Pollock's scribbles?
Meaningless to quibble over dribbles.

XXXIX

Wagner's Ring sings!
We *adore* every solo part!
If we could only bring the start
A bit nearer the end or exit before its beginnings!

XL

Queen Elizabeth the First
Presided over a golden age and the worst:
Of Shakespeare, Spenser and Marlowe,
Of black teeth, halitosis, gout and BO.

XLI

Sigmund Freud
Found his reputation destroyed
When he knocked off his mother
Then knocked up his father:
He may have been wearing the wrong specs
While rôle-playing his oedipus complex.

XLII

Jean-Baptiste-Camille Corot
Painted as though there were no tomorrow,
But much to his sorrow and to his great shame
His three thousand works look *exactly* the same.

XLIII

King Henry the Eighth
Hans Holbein portrayed in good faith.
That vast corporation with noble restraint
Still took nearly six tons of paint.

XLIV

Dr Livingstone, I presume, enchanted
As one of us is, I take it for granted
You must be he,
For it cannot be me
My judgment too heavily slanted.

XLV

Archimedes of Syracuse,
In his Turkish bath he changed a fuse
And observed that a saline solution
Helped to accelerate electrocution.

XLVI

When John Logie Baird invented television
It wasn't his vision to promote division
Between multiple viewers with multiple voices,
The downside of multiple choices.

XLVII

Oliver Cromwell's thoughts
Were totally absorbed by his warts.
In royal courts and health resorts
Ought his sort to be caught wearing shorts?

XLVIII

Niccolo Paganini's Caprices
Are exceedingly difficult pieces
On a harp in A-sharp for a harp seal
And quite an ordeal on a glockenspiel.

XLIX

Sir Francis Drake could hardly forsake
A game on the Hoe for the sake of an outbreak
Of typhoid, a world war, an earthquake
Or even the hint of a headache.

L

Howard of Effingham
Having a baldric he needed a wig,
He swore like a trooper and ate like a pig
And behaved like a regular Effing ham.

LI

Doctor Fu Manchu
Eschews shampoo.
His admirers clearly appreciate
The inestimable benefits of a greasy pate.

LII

Achilles' heel
Made it difficult to kneel.
When they shot off his kneecaps
It left him in total collapse.

LIII

Maria Montessori
Seldom felt hunky-dory.
Her vision for education
Fell short of inspiring a nation.

LIV

King George the First
Found his accent accurst
But his großvater's Erse
Was even worse.

LV

King George the Second
It has often been reckoned
Would have been more fecund
Had more mistresses beckoned.

LVI

King George the Third
Was only as good as his word,
And everybody garbles
When they start losing their marbles.

LVII

King George the Fourth
Made the long-dead Lord North
His future Prime Minister.
The move was considered quite sinister.

LVIII

King George the Fifth
Cared not who he was with.
When he married Queen Mary of Teck
He just said "Oh shucks, what the heck!"

LIX

King George the Sixth
Got most of his kicksth
By using his stammer
To hide his bad grammar.

LX

Queen Victoria
Gained a sense of euphoria
By splitting her drawers
While crouched on all fours.

LXI

Queen Victoria
Frequented Chinese Emporia.
Dim sum at the New York Astoria
Produced waves of severe logorrhoea.

LXII

King Henry the Eighth
Defender of the Faith,
Would have happily run a marathon
To escape Queen Catherine of Aragon.

LXIII

Elisha Otis
Got the sack at short notice
When his boss felt exceedingly miffed
Getting stuck in his own private lift.

LXIV

J.C. Bamford
Was recorded in Hansard
When he drove heavy plant
Through a Prime Ministerial rant.

LXV

Emperor Hirohito
Gave his geishas a floor show
When he lost his kimono
While going commando.

LXVI

King William the Fourth
Had his twopennorth
When the Great Reform Bill went
To receive his royal assent.

LXVII

King James the First
Among monarchs the worst,
But his "Counterblaste to Tobacco"
Left him bathed in a sententious afterglow.

LXVIII

King Charles the First
Was splendidly inhearsed
But first they chopped off his head
And made absolutely sure he was dead.

LXIX

Julius Caesar
Was a truculent geezer.
Once he'd subjugated the Gauls
He was left climbing the walls.

LXX

Henry Ford
Took their feelings on board
When his customers' feedback
Showed they all hated black.

LXXI

Franz Liszt
Was hardly missed
For not one composition
Was worthy of repetition.

LXXII

Caractacus
Wouldn't discuss
His treasonousness
Unless untrussed by Claudius.

LXXIII

Antonio Vivaldi
Would have got on with Garibaldi
For his music quite prettily
Unified Italy.

LXXIV

Viscount Melbourne
Considered himself so well-born
He was less than happy
To change his Princess's nappy.

LXXV

King John
Was proud to be part of the Bard's canon,
For he'd got it into his skull
That he was merely apocryphal.

LXXVI

Geoffrey Chaucer
Was prepared to divorce her
When he found the wife of Bath,
Was an eminent psychopath.

LXXVII

John Gower
Would glower and turn sour
When his "Confessio Amantis"
Was lost in Atlantis.

LXXVIII

Lawrence Sterne
Thought he could earn
More selling cough drops and candy
Than royalties from Tristram Shandy.

LXXIX

Alexander the Great
Would have carried less weight
Had he not had the bottle
To be coached by Aristotle.

LXXX

According to Wycliffe
Taking a quick spliff
Left his bible less
Liable to be libellous.

LXXXI

John Bunyan
Loved eating spring onion.
He failed to address
His pilgrims' distress.

LXXXII

Alexander Graham Bell
Could feel himself swell
When he invented the telephone
And put on twelve stone.

LXXXIII

John Keats's
Memorable feats
Fell short of pledges to burn
His "Ode to a Grecian Urn."

LXXXIV

Queen Marie Antoinette
Began to fret
When she made a loud cough
And her head fell off.

LXXXV

The Vicar of Bray
Said "Come what may
To Canterbury or Rome be all my praise
Conformist I'll be to the end of my days."

LXXXVI

John Huss
Would cuss and he'd fuss.
His mood took a nose-dive
When they burned him alive.

LXXXVII

Wenceslas Hollar
Always wore a Czech collar
But he violated Scots laws
When he wore tartan drawers.

LXXXVIII

Frederic Lord Leighton
Made his sitters put weight on.
When they still weren't fat enough
He put them up the duff.

LXXXIX

Elizabeth Gaskell
Was an insufferable rascal.
She created endless discord
By publishing "Cranford."

XC

Capability Brown
Achieved local renown
By concreting over his garden
To make his garden harden.

Part Two

Light
Before
the
Dawn

11 Clare

Clare

I

Hopes and a Misapprehension

A rosebud in a ribbon from her hair,
The most romantic gift with best intent
Spoke volumes more than she had ever meant
To say, more than she could have been aware.
It wore her scent, he thought it bore the care
She had for him and everywhere it went
With him, a symbol, rare and heaven-sent
Of what she was to him, and he to her.

But what *he* was had led him to presume
Too much in her: it ended on Hay Tor.
No shattered pride, a trait in him denied.
Though schoolboy vaunts his innocence belied,
As innocent among the purple broom
As she was he who wept up on the moor.

II

Beauty and a Rejection

Her carriage, femininity, her face
A perfect oval, her retroussé nose,
Exquisite as was she, the finest rose
Tints found in Eden's garden, and their place
It was to be, in dreams in timeless space.
He asked her, could she any time suppose
That she could love him? No, she said, she *knows*
She never could. He'd lost her, every trace

Of hope with her demolished at a whim.
Bewildered by her, he could only see
That thoughts so unequivocally shown
Would brook no plaintive argument from him:
She knew her own mind better far than he
And his mind better than she knew her own.

III

Beauty and Pathetic Fallacy

Thirty-six years ago they met and though
A child she seemed to him to be, yet one
Who showed sometimes the wisdom of Solon
Or Solomon. In such encounters so
Remote from earthliness do we forego
All mundane thought? Her beauty glowed upon
Her face and all about her bright light shone
More radiant by far than she could know.

The looming clouds rolled in, the bleak sun sank
To shroud in gloom the profile of the tor;
The gorse that spread by stealth had shed its bloom
But not its thorns, the tormentil was rank:
As innocent as she was he for whom
The clouds had gathered on the Devon moor.

IV

Innocence and Inexperience

For Farmer Boldwood one might well suspect
    Rejection was the hardest cross to bear.
    So like a death but with no body there,
    No carcase to collect with due respect
    Or disrespect, bereavement in effect
It was, for he was there and she elsewhere.
    Bathsheba, agent of his last despair
Yet of his deeds he was sole architect.

For blameless, how could *she* have known? No-one
    Could ever have foreseen the mischief done
By what seem harmless acts or words. Spellbound,
    Such power as he in helpless beauty found,
    Too blindly wrenched from solitude confined,
    Too soon restored, to solitude resigned.

V

Paradise Lost

It marks the psyche that it should exist
To temper instincts of its mortal host
With thought and reason and forbearance most
Of all. It counsels wisely to desist
When hope is lost, gives purpose to persist
When all is not. His being seemed almost
On borrowed time, so well her words engrossed
His thoughts, he fled before he was dismissed.

Regrets and memories of no avail
Though after all these years they still prevail.
Those barren hopeless days! Could he foresee
The ache, the solitude, how would it be?
Yet how could either happiness procure,
Her heart un-won and his left on the moor?

VI

One Letter

One letter only does he have from her.
Enclosure still intact it even now
Evokes those budding hopes, no matter how,
Forbidden thoughts unbidden still recur.
But memories invoke no blind despair
Since languor bears no dread: it can allow
But ennui and sleep. It seems somehow
The perfect state to be is unaware

As she, whose flawless beauty cannot be
Aware of what it is. It cannot see
Itself, it cannot see reflected what
We see in it nor feign what it is not.
Could he not feel the latent power in this,
The road to bliss that leads to the abyss?

VII

At Montacute House

It might have been a vacant wall they passed
Where sombrely those Tudor portraits hung,
And had the ghosts of Byrd or Tallis sung
For all to hear he would have been the last
To heed. If only lessons from the past
With sound precepts in action or by tongue
Could mitigate the progress of the young!
Their path is desert and the desert vast.

Dutch gables, ogee roofs, no gloomy towers;
How could Renaissance architecture blow
In dialogue those all too precious hours
Among what few remained? He could not know.
While youth is wasted on the young we're told
The hopes of youth are wasted on the old.

VIII

The Burden of Memory

The joys upon this earth that we proclaim
Will pass like those that we've already had.
Our memories must ipso facto all be sad,
Not being in the here and now, what came
Has gone away, the past we can't reclaim.
And as Mark Antony declaimed, while bad
Deeds bring men shame, who make them glad
May not receive their well-deserved acclaim.

Remembrances, those moments undismissed,
Can only hamper healing. Bring about
The Devon moor eternal night, combine
It with impenetrable constant mist,
Then might he say that "out of sight is out
Of mind, and she forever out of mine."

IX

Unspoken Words

Down all these years what memories remain
To haunt as deeply as they did before?
The things we should have said and didn't; more
Than what we've done it's all that we complain
We should have done while sadly we maintain
The status quo. Why did he set such store
By unconsidered words? And yet *ignore*
Them he could not: such questions are in vain.

If wrongs could all be righted and our crimes
Erased (and some committed many times)
Yet his would need the greatest clemency:
More beauty in this world he'd never see
Again, he always knew, yet on that day
He went away he didn't even say.

X

A Return to the Moor

And half a lifetime was to pass before
He saw Hay Tor again. Did hapless doom
Dictate it thus and from the very womb?
How could it be so little and no more,
That first love he had waited so long for?
From full bloom to the pallor of the tomb,
The memories he never need exhume,
They lie unburied on the Devon moor.

The autumn now: encroaching bracken, bent
Grass and the withered fescue round the tor
And where the thready tormentil once lay
The birds were silent and the summer spent,
And something died upon the moor that day
Still-born, the day it died upon the moor.

12 Dina
&
MND

Mourning Sickness

Can anybody say how long it lasts,
This numbness that deceives while it relieves
The harrowed brain? My senseless state contrasts
So markedly with that of he who grieves
In honest but conventional display,
In typecast manner, equally sincere,
But may I say, the day she passed away,
Was pity any help to her to hear?

Exemplars for my silence may be found:
Few patterns for my infinite regret.
Excuses plead for me, the words compound
The pain I gave her, how can I forget?
Bring joy to her and clemency to me,
My soul with hers? If only that could be!

Dying at Home

They let her die at home. It meant less stress,
Less artificial bright-and-breeziness
From health professionals who can't confess
Cant won't dispel a patient's queasiness.

They pander to our vain deluded hopes,
Their best prognoses worse than horoscopes,
And though sometimes they may extend our years
So seldom can they mitigate our tears.

With stethoscope and specs around their necks
The doctors say her time has sadly come.
This much she knows, and this what she expects:
To certainties she cannot but succumb.

For some the cri de coeur to die transcends
The moral qualms to which she need not bow:
Without the means to compass our own ends
Can we be guilty just for knowing how?

No power had she to perish or persist,
To go beyond the brink, abandon me.
So hard sometimes to think we can exist
A unilateral dependency.

She could not eat, nor could she longer speak,
Fed through a tube, could neither bite nor chew.
Too bleak the scene, to bleat or weep, too weak
Was she to see another morning dew!

This mourning due? Bereavement yet unborne.
Catharsis it may bring to some, not me.
Forlorn I feel, forlorn and battle-worn
And yet I cannot mourn, it cannot be.

A mind refined, so kind was she, inclined
To find the best in me; I was at first
The best for her, so cursed was she, resigned
At last to find in me the very worst?

I cannot say just why I cannot grieve.
A trumped-up rage supplants my wretchedness,
That she should drift to sleep so soon and leave
Me unprepared for this expectedness.

A little late it is, I think, to say
I prized her for her troubles lightly worn,
And bigger burdens bravely borne. This day
Is blank for me and lifeless is the dawn.

Though scarcely could she move her head yet she
Brought dignity and courage with each breath.
For all her trials there must surely be
A special place to take her after death.

If only I could help her as I should,
My own faults legion, I would simply fail:
She knew I would have helped her if I could,
But my attempts were all to no avail.

So often in great pain was she that night
(And how refined her torments were!) she was
Incapable of pointing to the site.
She could not say how much it hurt because

At last she lost the remnant of her voice.
Too faint by now to tell me where each pain
She suffered hurt, it left her with no choice:
Remain in pain, complain again in vain.

All through the dreary night her throat was raw,
She dared not drink at all for she could not
Take any liquid in, nor even draw
It through a straw. That night she was too hot,

Sometimes she was too cold: We tried to set
The thermostat; to what, she could not say.
Sometimes she'd sleep and, let us hope, forget
The trials of her waking hours for they

Were filled with aches, discomfort, restlessness
While in and out of consciousness, a state
That alternated with her breathlessness,
And fleeting moments would alleviate.

And sometimes she was in a darker place
Than that in which she lay; where sadly we
Would hear her most despondent cries: her face
Wore every sorrow that could ever be.

Sometimes, frustrated by her helplessness,
Her cries, so lonely and so desolate;
Their trigger, difficult to try to guess,
Too terrible to even contemplate.

Her aches grew worse and worse as it grew late,
For pain relief she gave me no assent,
I talked to her, I tried to cope with great
And sorrowful and piteous lament.

And someone else was in the room that night
Unseen by me yet charged with light and prone
Like the ascetic or the eremite
To wander in the desert all alone.

And in the land of Abraham and Job
That stick He bore would probe the arid sand,
His woollen shawl withal His linen robe,
His sandals and His girdle lightly tanned.

Her sun will surely rise in brighter skies.
She lay, worn out by life, her labours done.
And long before the morning light her eyes
Were closed, no tears from her and mine were gone.

No kinder woman in the human race,
I wished I could have lain there in her place
Or could have done more to allay the strife
That constantly beset her mortal life.

Portents and Tributes

We trust she found the Christ she sighed to see
Whom Judas sold, another man denied,
The Golden Gate, the Sea of Galilee,
Mount Calvary where he was crucified,
The shadow of the cross upon the wall
In Nazareth, death's portent in the room.*
Blood-red the moon at noon, and over all
The blackest pall where Christ broke from
His tomb.

Profound the peace that fills this hallowed ground
For here in ancient Aramaic script
A tribute scrawled upon the shifting sand
And strewn about and all around and slipped
Among the flowers on her grave we found
Madonna lilies from the Holy Land.

vide "The Shadow of Death"
by William Holman Hunt

293

I Only Knew

I only knew, beside her where I sat,
Her smile for me would last a thousand years.
So much to say to her as daybreak nears
Not then and in our place and habitat
Did we feel any urgency for that.
As eyesight fails internal vision clears.
But now she's dead and no more sees nor hears
I never knew the world could be so flat.

And she deserves my sorrow and my tears,
Deserves them all through my remaining years,
Deserves to know I think of her and grieve.
Though she receive no pity please believe
My sadness lies unsought upon the shelf
Because she bore no pity for herself.

Poles Apart

Unlike the grin upon the Cheshire Cat
Her smile, remembered, cannot ever pall.
Why such disastrous evils should befall
A creature kind as she, so noble that
In dispute peacemaker and diplomat
Until her last day and her own nightfall
A free-for-all, her heart on call to all,
And when she went we found the earth was flat.

Why did she go and leave me here below?
We know too well the reason why: for though
I would have chased her up Mount Erebus
Or to the bottom of the Barents Sea
There never could have been the two of us,
To Eden she and Erebus for me.

The Light Before the Dawn

That night a being shone with perfect light,
Unseen by me but for an aura quite
Ethereal, eclipsing all in sight
Of the unearthly fire within. I might
Have seen by proxy what she saw: despite
Her trials recognition in her sight
For in her eyes I saw the fires ignite
Her spirit for her soul's immortal flight.

By dawn her soul had found a brighter light,
But had I been a truly awful blight
Upon her troubled life would it be right
To pray that she and I might reunite?
Her eyes shone with the crescent moon that night,
So bright they were, so very very bright.

Gdansk

We made landfall in Poland for the last
Fog-laden hours we ever spent abroad,
A chilly April day and overcast.
The Long Market: how could I have ignored
Those ancient dwellings riding on the mist
In pastel hues, like houseboats all afloat?
The mist poured on the ground, hard to resist
The other-worldly scene: frock-coat to throat,

A stallman stood, in fustian, cocked hat,
And called to me, Great God! And so did she!
Day-dreaming I, while she had fallen flat.
But had we known that she had MND,
I would have sped to her in awful dread,
And reached her long before the pigeons fled.

Gdansk Revisited

Her cry shattered the silence on the pier.
I heard her call my name from where she fell,
Where pigeons fed on shreds of bread don't fear
Stray dogs and mogs but scattered at her yell.
Some fled and some in dread prepared to flee,
Their clatter fills the air, still they are free,
These hordes of pigeons, free like you and me,
As she, by God's decree, could never be.

In scholarship immersed and so well versed,
And artless too, her actions unrehearsed,
Her nous might have achieved a double first
Where now she lies as only one accursed.
A tumour on the brain she thought at first
She had and some time later heard the worst.

A Wheelchair

They kept their car-doors shut and windows closed,
Nor left their house but stayed inside, disposed
To hide if D were waiting wheelchair-bound
Outside. Attendant crew, no siren sound,

The ambulance would call and she would stay
Away all day in hospital and they
Would never know the reason she was there:
They wouldn't know: of course they wouldn't care.

They couldn't know or tell that this appointment
Would go so well or spell flat disappointment,
Might aid research. A triallist she was,
She wanted to save other lives because

Despite these ventures into the unknown,
She couldn't ever hope to save her own.
Her neighbours on both sides of her were kind:
They proffered all their help and hoped they'd find

A cure, a remedy for MND.
It's just what we would really like to see.
Across the road, though, opposite to me
An attitude far simpler to foresee.

For they would think themselves quite neighbourly
In living scarcely forty feet from me,
And "keeping themselves to themselves," you see,
While living here in such propinquity.

How *is* this neighbourly? How do we sleep
At night? How righteous it is to keep
Ourselves so utterly, completely to
Ourselves and make a virtue of it too?

A hazard on the pavements they might say?
At any rate they shunned her till the day
She died. I wonder was that wheelchair why
They stayed away and never said goodbye?

And when the ramp was taken up outside
Our house they surely wondered had she died,
And still I wonder why, it's such a shame,
They never knew she died, they never came.

Once ably used, now purposeless instead,
That handy wheelchair in the garden shed
She drove it once with skill, full steam ahead,
Round corridors in hospitals she sped.

That empty wheelchair in the garden shed
She drove it like a sled and fast she sped,
So animated once it used to be,
So poignant now it looks and dead as she.

And she was safe. Outdoors she seemed to flow
Round corners; indoors she was wont to show
Facility, manoeuvrability
And all despite her disability.

Too soon alas her illness passed the stage
Where she could drive that wheelchair to assuage
The loss of her ability to drive
A car, one tiny reason to survive

Until she lost the strength to stay alive.
No tiny movement left to her, all gone
Down to her fingertips, could no more strive
To stay alive, could no more carry on.

And though her illness drained mobility:
She never lost her sensitivity
And took it sadly when, in her wheelchair,
She'd be ignored as though she were not there.

And opposite, our neighbours would lie low,
Would not emerge to speak to her, to show
How she could die these several months ago
So close to them and yet they didn't know.

That wheelchair looked so doleful to my sight
Detached it was, as she, from humankind.
And wheelchair-bound,
they shunned her morn till night.
I hope it served to bring them peace of mind.

A precious life is gone, too late to care,
To treat her as an entity, resigned
As she to being part of that wheelchair:
Not neighbourly enough to have a mind

To come and speak to us, the less they knew
The better. Never poke or pry in case
Afflicted neighbours ask for help from you,
When all you want to do is give them space.

Afflicted neighbours, friends in need, are friends
That we can do without. Our need transcends
All things: on this our happiness depends
And dealing with our own reaps dividends.

That's why they never came to speak and why
They never cared enough to say goodbye.

Shared Memories

Her death should terminate the times we had
Together, all our prospects, all we planned
For these are gone like footprints in the sand.
And yet the memories will make me glad
To know that what remains is not as sad
As I expect. For now I understand
How could my loss of her bring back first-hand
Recall of all the good times not the bad.

I'd always left shared memories with her
For me to plunder as and when I would
And these her nature filtered for the good.
Her steadfast presence gone from next to where
I stood her death could never rob our past,
I know, of all those memories amassed.

A Misunderstanding

Supposing she had more self-pity would
I too have had more pity for her plight?
Did others' pity do her any good?
She spared none for herself upon that night
And only intermittently she slept
And poorly through the pain but when she did
I knew for certain that she never wept:
Her tears nor she nor any could have hid.

But then, before her voice completely failed,
Though paralysed in all her limbs, not dead
But fading fast, before she died she wailed
From far beyond us both it seemed. I said
"Don't cry like that," but she misunderstood.
She said it was the only way she could.

A Time for Sorrow

Today already six months down the line
Yet after all this time I barely feel
That I am ready to begin to heal.
A deadline for my grief? Can you assign
A time for sorrow, grieving by design,
Precise as lightning, cold as carbon steel,
As certain as the ceaseless balance wheel
That regulates your beating heart and mine?

But why forget? Why would I want to lose
Recall of all I know of one whose smiles
And ringing laughter carried me for miles
Around the earth? If I could pick and choose
Our memories not one would I destroy,
I'd save them all and every jot of joy.

The Courage of a Lion

I wish I'd told her long ago how brave
She was before quietus, her godsend.
Her lion's heart insisted that she spend
Last Christmas dying but alive, to stave
Off death that day and spare her children, save
Her grandchildren, by force of will contend
With her extinction and delay the end
To mitigate their pain beyond her grave.

A sad end met the courage she displayed
Yet this was one more way she proved her worth,
And nothing did she covet on this earth
But happiness in others she purveyed.
Now all around her know she truly found
Her peaceful ground aloft by heaven bound.

Passing Passerines

Though next to human woe so trite I know,
But birds sustain, like us, hard lives. In strife
They live, as do all earthbound things below.
The sparrow is the subject of a life.
Can anything be more important to
A sparrow than its self? The worm that delves
To balk the shrew, so too the tiny shrew
To balk the hawk, all fending for their selves.

And though the sparrow lives and dies in fear
The closure of its rôle as constant prey
Perhaps itself imparts some comfort here,
Some kind of instant anaesthetic spray.
A painful end for innocents is odd,
Not one we'd like inflicted by *our* God.

No Longer There

I wonder if a change has come about.
No longer do I feel that she is there
As physical a being in her chair
To me as I to her. My words ring out
And they receive no answer but they flout
The silence of the grave. I'm still aware
Her presence thwarts self-pity and despair:
Her spirit still bedecks the house throughout

With declarations that her goodness wore
And every kindness that set her apart
From you and me. Each day I thank God for
Her warmth and for the wellspring of her heart.
I like to think her soul, unknown to vice
Is welcome this day forth in Paradise.

Between Life and Death

As frail as gossamer and just as thin
The line that marks the living world we're in
From those once with us who now lie within
Their graves. So hard to take upon the chin
Is not death but the being dead: wherein
Our earthly strife is followed by what sin
Has earned for us, it seems we cannot win,
Our pains are over, let the new begin.

But some there are whose kindness on this earth
Must give free passage for their priceless worth.
That horse's tail hair gave her no unease
From which depends the sword of Damocles.
Be sure from hell on earth her boundless love
Led straight to glory and the realm above.

Now Let Her Rest in Peace

Now let her rest in peace, though neither will
Nor wits take flight. With lambent gaze and bright
Intelligence, with her profound insight,
Her skull repository of such skill.
A death sentence suspended only till
The mask is off, so to her onward flight;
The sterile room that staged her desperate fight
To draw each breath an image with us still.

When these infernal bellows cease to send
Her measured gasps of air her hours are done,
And all her earthly labours at an end.
The world goes on but she'll be dead and gone,
So let her wisdom shine this one last night
And in the morning take away the light.

How Resolute are
the Condemned

How resolute are the condemned and how
Their courage overtops their burning fear!
As I till this, though in our fifteenth year,
Had never seen such valour to avow,
Or anyone whose mettle I should bow
To and revere or something very near:
To step into the darkest night from here,
And leave her place among the living now.

That she'd be gone before the dawn she knew,
A knowledge she alone was privy to.
Yet she, beyond belief, beyond compare
Came home to me, away from nursing care.
Her fears she must have taken to the grave:
Without them she could not have been so brave.

Worldly Wealth

For worldly wealth she really didn't care
And her possessions mostly simply made,
Her dying sister's ragged teddy bear
She tenderly conveyed from Adelaide.
A wedding ring she had, the rest was bling,
A few pathetic little bits of paste,
And worthless costume jewels, nor anything
Could ever make her flaunt expensive taste.

They all survived her though her caritas
Lives on. I must let go the things she had,
Each tired and tawdry item. Yet so sad,
These relics are, unworldly vanitas.
With feelings raw as this so hard somehow,
Though someday soon I really must, not now.

Memory

Sometimes I look and she is there with me,
A cushion, throw or rug enough to mark
Or represent her presence in the dark.
I know, because I have been told, I'll see
Her less and less as time goes by and she,
As memory goes frail and as the spark
Of fireflies fainter grows, the mounting lark
With height, the sight of her to me will be.

The failing memory is our release,
And nature cannot make us suffer more
On earth than we are able to endure.
Cold comfort though, for she had little peace.
But sure of this I am, her final breath
Swept her to glory with a fearless death.

Not a Sparrow Falls

A portent for our loss, this bird, so nigh
Its end. The slowly creeping dusk had dared
It to emerge, its doughty spirit bared,
Eyes bright as lightning in a sullen sky.
The lesser creature never questions why
It lives in constant fear nor why a bird
Must needs defend a life it never cared
To own. For birds don't ask to live or die.

Nor she, As heaven-sent so heavenward
She went. And how on earth did she afford,
In midst of her own dying, empathy?
As modesty denied her charity:
For kindly deeds she wrought but nought professed
We now commend her spirit with the blest.

While Sitting by Her

While sitting by her sometimes I would eye
Her dext'rous fingers plying to and fro
While unbeknown to her, as she would sew
And crochet, knit and stitch and satisfy
Her urge to work for charity, defy
Approaching death with kindness. So although
She had to go, yet why I didn't know.
I sat beside her and I wondered why.

Meanwhile her fingers plying to and fro
Had been the final part of her to go.
And when her fingers went her work was done.
Before all feeling bar the pain had gone
Those instruments of charity and love,
Her hands, he surely guided from above.

Virtue its Own Reward

How well her unremitting kindness stands
As witness all her labour making toys
And clothes for disadvantaged children, boys
In wretched deprivation, threads for bands
Of hapless youths. Her never-idle hands
Would bring her self-fulfilment, helpless joys
Her selfless ploys still sing as she enjoys
The happiness her kindest care commands.

Agnostic she, no gain in prospect for
Her ceaseless cause to benefit the poor.
On Judgment Day no punishment sublime,
No God, no trial, heaven or hell to fight.
But not for her the dreary weight of time,
The bleak and barren coldness of the night.

Her Hands

Her fingers worked incessantly all through
Her waking hours to benefit the poor,
Her needlecraft deployed not as a chore
But from an almost helpless need to do
What she could do in order to pursue
The happiness of you and me. She wore
The most infectious smile while still she bore
Much more upon her shoulders than her due.

To find those little hands of hers as we
So rarely saw them, motionless; to see
Her sadness in the knowledge there could be
No more that she could do for you or me.
Despite the pathos she would no more balk
At awful fate than take her bed and walk.

It Seems so Brutal

Cremation seems a brutal way to end
Our sojourn here; no time to reappraise
Our ways, our apologia, rephrase
Our vicious injudicious words, pretend
Our differences did not exist, befriend
Imagined foes, misspend our precious days,
And, like the thief on Calvary, it pays
If we confess our wrongs right at the end.

Give us the cold earth and a quiet grave,
A tiny space to call our own, to wave
Goodbye and while we decompose rejoice
For our immortal soul. The other choice,
The crematorium, the past a flash:
Our spirits all will long survive our ash.

Till We Care Too Much

Sometimes it seems we keep them till we care
Too much and then what happens next? Why! They
Are snatched away from us. She couldn't stay,
I cannot go. It fills me with despair
That while I'm here I cannot be with her.
Each night a ready meal or takeaway
And I'll sit here where I sit every day
To eat but no-one will be sitting where

She sat nor will again to smile at me,
Agree or (with sound reason) disagree
With me in bearing news or airing views,
Opinions to gainsay or peruse.
Our thoughts alone we can't profess:
If no-one hears they're pointless to express.

Motor Neurone Disease

This long slow dying is the worst of all,
And all that waiting hour by hour for each
New symptom, each new body-blow to fall.
What she needs now is far beyond our reach,
To halt the march of this paralysis.
Designed for vibrant life was she, consigned
To death, yet in the last analysis
No cure ahead leaves hope and prayer behind.

And this is how God sometimes takes His own,
He blights them in their prime. See how she strives
Against the choking breathlessness alone,
This horrible disease that none survives.
How odd of God to blight them in their prime:
How sad to see them die before their time.

She Left Her Home

She left her home, career, her life for me,
We heeded not and little cared how deep
The gulf before us yawned. A massive leap
Of faith, how wide a chasm could it be?
She seldom of her nature let me see
When she was tried or found it hard to keep
Her even tenor. Whirlwinds might she reap
Nor make complaint to others or to me.

I mind sometimes I was unkind to her.
Henceforth I will deserve her loyal care.
Why let her go because she ceased to be,
To leave forever all but memory?
I took her hand in mine and now I know
I wish that I had never let it go.

No Return

How fine we felt while round the world we went,
    We'd feast on all those fifteen fleeting years!
    At photos from long past the present peers,
        Each picosecond's flash a real event
    In time. Forgive those failings that give vent
    To present tears, forget my future fears.
    Cold comfort my desert, it little cheers
    Me, wronging her, to know I better meant.

    And even as the days flowed by we'd yearn
        To end the now, relive some other time,
    The present spurn, the past our sole concern;
    Nor sought the sights of Eden's heights sublime.
    Too late, when earthbound time is done, we learn
        That we can leave but never can return.

While Waiting
through the Night

This morning, searching on the laptop, I
Found notes I made upon the night she died.
All through the darkest hours at her bedside
That night I knew she knew her end was nigh.
And in the morning light though she would lie
There still, at peace, in death so dignified,
Between us both would be a gulf so wide
When she was gone and I would wonder why.

And still would she be lying alongside
And I would look at her: she could not see.
And I would speak: she could not answer me.
And I would hope: but no-one heard my plea.
And still she lay there, silent and dry-eyed,
And still would I be grieving by her side.

The Curlew and the Lark

On rare days baked in sunlight, bogward bound
The gaudy sight of heather on the hill.
The curvirostral curlew couldn't kill
With such a bill but will, its sound renowned,
Announce itself. It doesn't hang around
To hearken to the lark or mark it spill
Its liquid notes from tiny lungs to fill
The air with music tumbling to the ground.

Unlike the lark are we, it seems to me.
We have no wings, we are not free to flee
This earth except we our quietus make.
If only we could sleep and not awake
If we can never be with those we love
Again, nor ever see them up above.

Panic

What is this feeling that sometimes afflicts
Us with awful intensity and fear?
A feeling close to panic, very near
To dread, to terror; something that constricts
The breathing, chokes the throat and lungs, inflicts
Its toll in sleepless nights and days of sheer
And utter misery, when fiends appear
Before us though our reason contradicts

Their presence here. From hell they come, where do
They go? They tell us that we'll not behold
Belovèd ones again, though we bestrew
The way with lilies, rubies and white gold:
For only hope and prayer avail us then
And God alone can tell us if and when.

So Much Unsaid

So much unsaid, though we both knew how too
Few hours she lingered on this earth, to show
I cared for her. How had I let her go,
Nor begged He bring her back as she withdrew
From me? Affection with affliction grew
Till she, too weak, no longer could bestow
Her kindness. Still her love would overflow
But I, too blind to both, I barely knew.

So beautiful in death. Her mind lives on
Though she can no more hear nor speak nor see.
Too late for reassurance now she's gone,
To give the little that she asked of me.
In memory must I maintain her trust,
And soon may mine be mingled with her dust.

If Only I had Cared for Her

If only I had cared for her as I
Care for her now that she is dead and done.
If only I had told her that, though none
As undemonstrative as I, yet why
Did I not tell her then though I would fly
To her and seize her now that she is gone?
If only one day we could be as one,
If only I might find her when I die.

If only I might make amends for black
And gloomy moods, to beg that she forgive
My lack of feeling, ask that she come back
To me who can no longer bear to live
Without her constant presence by my side.
If only it were both of us that died.

Why Do I Know

Why do I know her better now she's gone?
Why should her precious memory be so
Much brighter than the she I used to know,
Much stronger to me now her time is done?
Through kindly words and deeds she lingers on
Nor could be won by death. How should she go?
For now my eyes have opened I would show
Her none could ever love her more, not one.

Why did she suffer, why grossly maligned
Was she, for helping me through blackest days,
By one who really ought to have been kind
To her, deserving nothing but her praise?
Entrenched her bigotry, a woman who
Saw none but her own twisted point of view.

The Hebrides

She never saw the Hebrides, nor could
She see St Kilda from the ashen screes
Of Eaval or the Harris hills, from these
The furthest isles, to see them where they stood
Amid the roiling North Atlantic seas that flood
Our shores each day, whose far horizon frees
Our thoughts of heartache and the mind's disease,
And leads us in our dreams to where we would.

I wish I'd taken her so long ago.
It's where she wanted to go, that I know.
And now I sit here wishing she could be
Upon the Isle of Skye with me and see
Her dog's big ears flapping in the breeze,
If only she had seen the Hebrides.

The Three of Us

I

So long ago it is to call to mind
When she and he and I were here, we three.
It must have been a happy place to be,
Her cocker spaniel almost designed
To fill the dog-shaped space that we assigned
To him beside the hearth. And full of glee
Was he to be with her if it were she
Or be with me, no need he for his kind.

And then he died and we would never buy
Another dog for who could take his place?
Nor dog nor any beast could even try,
And none, it seemed, among the human race.
And we might search the earth and still we'd find
That none could fill the space he left behind.

II

And surely, for we loved him, God will find
A place for him to be with us, the three
Of us. For indivisible were we.
More innocent than any of our kind
Was he, we couldn't leave the dog behind.
He brought to us the greatest joy to see
His happiness, and he designed to be
Upon the moor and running unconfined.

They came to put him down and he lay calm
In Dina's lap, and still he wagged his tail
And knew we wouldn't do him any harm
Whose joyful life could never countervail
For us against the sorrow of his loss
Who nevermore would roam upon the moss.

III

And then there were just two of us and part
Of each of us had died with him. No more
Could we walk anywhere we'd gone before
Together. Neither of us had the heart
To wander those old ways again, to start
Once more to roam the stones upon the moor.
The happy world we lived in was no more,
The life that we had shared had come apart.

We three were one, but now she too is gone
This feeling all alone and lost, for none
Can ever fill her space now she is dead.
And only dread keeps me from my deathbed
And I live on, endure a living curse
For fear alone of something even worse.

IV

Her spirit still goes on though she is gone
From me, and my dependence on her shorn
Forever though it felt that we were born
To be together, three of us as one.
When first we met that day the bright sun shone
Upon the morn, though bitter chill the dawn.
And when she died and I was left to mourn
I only wished, like hers, my life were done.

The time we had together all too brief,
Those fifteen years. She warrants all my grief
And I would leave this earth forthwith to see
If I could find her, bring her home to me.
Our grief a heavy price we pay for love,
Unless, pray God, we meet again above.

V

They both are gone and I am left behind,
  Reminded how it feels to be alone
And wake up every morning on my own,
  When all that I can hope for is to find
That I can still bring both of them to mind,
  On black and dismal days when I bemoan
My loss, to think at least that I have known
  Them both gives solace to a mind resigned

To wait here till the day that we can be
  Together once again, to know that we
Were happy once, to feel the being blest.
  The pity would be thinking all our best
Days are behind us, days we were enthralled
  To be alive could never be recalled.

VI

There must be worse or better times to come
For otherwise why would we be acquainted
With knowledge of what's good and evil, tainted
With atavistic dread? Afraid that some
Of us are bound for hell where we succumb
To torments. Not for her, among His sainted
Ones, but for whited sepulchres and painted
Women, thieves, liars. Better deaf and dumb

Were they who drip gall and calumniate
Their betters and engage in billingsgate.
If only I could henceforth try to live
As she, whose words to me revealed her love,
Whose charity alone must surely give
To her free passage to the realms above.

Autumn Thoughts

Two years ago she went away and here
I sit alone and wait for her each day.
And sometimes I am angry at the way
That she was taken from me. Crystal clear
Her memory, though withered now and sere,
The herbs are leafless, dwindle and decay.
Enchanted but forlorn the thorn, the may
We planted, in the half-light dim and drear.

The roof-tiles lichened, dripping wet the eaves,
The guttering is full of rotting leaves,
The ground is sodden all around, across
The lawn the grass has yielded to the moss.
I sit here wretched, staring at the walls,
It's dark at three, and no-one ever calls.

December

Two years ago it didn't seem as cold
As this. But then her heart was warm, and she
Would make this house a happy place to be.
Where once the rhododendron would unfold
The garden weeds exert their stranglehold.
The lawn is sodden wet, the rowan tree
Has shed its showy berries. Here we see
Its boughs are bare, so barren to behold.

The dying and the dead surround me here
Till in the spring the flowers reappear
In all their glory as they do each year
To bring us happiness and bring us cheer.
But still I mourn in this December chill
For she will not come back, nor ever will.

In Articulo Mortis

How were those final moments, were they fraught
With pain? Not at the end. Nor was there dread
Upon her face that saw what lay ahead.
And there were two of us before, then nought
But one, for she had fought her Agincourt
And gone. And at the last she seemed to shed
Life wholly reconciled to being dead
For she had found the light her goodness sought.

For all her trials here at peace she lay,
Serene her end, it seemed, a sacred death.
Light years away from here I heard her say
Goodbye to me and with her dying breath
She left her life, her past, she left me too,
And all she had and all she ever knew.

13 MND & Me

Dina

I

A Terminal Illness

How will I cope when she's no longer there?
Dependence all too easy to resent
When her support is gone; more to lament
To find we have another cross to bear,
An added burden to a loss. Unfair
To her it seems to be. Should I repent
My compromising grief in giving vent
To pity for *myself* in *her* despair?

But mourning her reliability
Is not a sorrow that I ought to spare,
Because my grieving that lost quality
Of hers must also mean I grieve for *her.*
Her steadfastness nobody could outdo,
In missing this of course I'll miss her too.

II

The Leaden Silence

How will I live with her not here to speak
To me? Already while she is away
From home in hospital I cannot say
How leaden has the silence been. Last week
We heard the devastating news, as bleak
As it could be, and nothing can convey
The sorrow, nothing can allay the way
It feels. Unlike were we but sympathique,

And quick was I to rile, she quicker yet
To smile; impulsive she, so unlike me;
Reserved was I and slower to forget;
Open her thoughts, mine under lock and key.
Why do I speak already in the past?
Because our present is too short to last.

III

Contrition

How will I feel, alone, when she is gone?
I cannot know but I can only fear
The worst, the memory, remorse, sincere
Regret still lingers. How can I move on?
How can I be at peace with her, at one
With her as she, I trust, to Him is near?
The recollection will stay crystal clear
If I remembered nothing else I've done.

One day impatiently our door I shut
While still she stood upon the threshold but
I don't think that I knew she was still there.
So weak, she fell. So too the mask she'd wear.
The once alone throughout our time that she
Broke down and cried, she cried because of me.

IV

The Pathos in the Trivial

What else will I recall and what forget?
Impossible to second-guess, to find
Which memories will press upon the mind,
So whimsical the things that most upset.
The pathos in the trivial may set
Me grieving most, those little aches inclined
To let the bigger tag along behind.
And yet they too perpetuate regret.

Those little things that gave us little thought,
Inconsequential acts and things undone
Whose memories in grief we never sought
And these I will turn over one by one,
And think of how my time has overrun,
Of one that's gone, not one that was unwon.

V

Hope in Despair

How will I smile again without her here?
This short time on my own has been a taste,
A foretaste, of a future laid to waste.
For me I think the worst thing is, I fear
The silence every day and year on year;
It's not the quiet serenity that laced
Our dialogue, nor peace at night that spaced
Our days, but this, the silence of despair.

Soon would we know what quiet courage died
With her; The patience that would manifest
Itself though she was long and sorely tried,
The wisdom to leave censure unexpressed,
Her charity of virtues unsurpassed
And childlike trust that hope prevails at last.

VI

A Half-Read Book

There's something so affecting in the sight
 Of that unfinished book upon the floor
As if, should I wait long enough, the door
Could open and without a sound she might
Return to me from far beyond the night,
 Sit down exactly where she sat before
And read again. How long could I abjure
The darkness for or she abhor the light?

Before the bookmark at that page she thrives
 In memory for kindly words she said,
For deeds she wrought, for those whose hapless lives
She bettered while her own she left unread.
Beyond that page it still cuts like a knife,
That suffering should drain her mortal life.

VII

Requiescat in Pace

So to the dying embers of the day
Our sight no longer bounded by the light.
The mind's eye finds why western skies delight
In blushes, heaven-born each lambent ray.
Her life adorned by trials one might say:
Though sorrows give the psyche no respite
With courage borne it flies to untold height
From cares released when shorn of mortal clay.

And when the deep veil drops on each and all
For this our judgment here we stand or fall
Alone. "In manus tuas Domine,"
Her time has come, so too the fatal day.
Lord, lead her bravely out of this dark night
To greet a new dawn, glorious and bright.

The Demons of the Night

All since she left me I have lived in fear
Of creatures dwelling in the shadows here,
And all around and pressing into me
With pallid faces I can scarcely see.

For they are hooded and a sickly grey
Who never any malice will betray,
Though dark as night are they, from head to foot,
Their eyes like coals, their clothes as black as soot.

And if I ask one of these goths to show
The way to go it seems he does not know.
They never answer me, and should I shout
That I am lost they simply turn about,

And never do they make a single sound,
But blocking me they always stand their ground.
Profoundly deaf are they and mute, I think.
They must be blind, it seems, they do not blink.

But there was never any need to skirt
Around these ghostly figures or avert
Them. I could step right through them to reveal
That nothing but the night did they conceal.

And sometimes I would be aboard a barque,
An old square-rigger like the Cutty Sark,
Along dark passages below I'd flee,
And through the ports would be the angry sea.

And somewhere in the house I'd stand aghast
In some vast auditorium, harassed
By adolescents standing cloaked in black
In black-upholstered tipping seats pushed back.

And in the dark I'd try to find a sign,
Of something I might recognise, a line
That I could draw between reality
And what I thought I saw but couldn't see.

The ceiling coved or open to the sky
And it was always cold and I would try
To find of my possessions some small sign,
To find something I recognised as mine.

And once I found I was upon a train
And bitter chill it was, in freezing rain,
It traversed many miles in my own home
The tarmac of a disused aerodrome.

And trackless, here and there the train would go,
Pull into stations that I didn't know,
And back and forth we'd go and never could
I see a soul and never thought I would.

And on we went, flat fields to either hand,
With mud and gravel, puddles, bleak the land.
So long ago the hawthorns' leaves had shed.
Their twisted branches spiked the air ahead.

We stopped beside a platform dark and drear,
And here a group of people huddled near
The ticket office. None got on and none
Got off the train but I the only one.

And in the waiting room I saw a light
Switch on the wall. I turned it on, so bright
It was and in the light I saw the hall,
And there a pair of shoes against the wall.

And on the mat a letter with my own
Address on it and from the telephone
Upon the table by the door I'd see
That I was home and where I ought to be.

It rained all night: why were the carpets dry?
And why no trace of peat-black earth, and why
No stamp of tramping feet led from the door
In sodden clags of mud across the floor?

And sinister and strange it is to be
Incarcerated in the day yet free
To walk the night, to stalk the living dead
While still I breathe and with the living tread.

If I could only bring her home with me
The demons of the night would surely flee
This house, and no more would I ever dread
The night nor ever fear the living dead.

14 A Fortunate Few

Jessica

I

The Die was Cast

Their tresses were alike, should he forget,
That lustrous hair for which Jane Morris sat
To captivate Rossetti; those brunette
And auburn waves and curls and ringlets that
Would tumble round the roses of her face.
They sang together in the Salford choir,
Her voice a clear soprano, his a bass:
It might have been Die Schöpfung or Messiah

That they sang, but there the die was cast,
Their course already fixed. He asked her could
He paint her, as Rossetti might have asked.
She acquiesced, he painted her, that should
Have been an end: instead what had begun?
Some things, if only they might be undone!

II

Reason to Live

For her sake he could wish they hadn't met,
　For his sake what a mercy that they did.
　An orthopaedic surgeon might have set
　His broken bones, a neurosurgeon rid
　His brain of haemorrhage, but only she
Could mend a broken life and help him strive
　To climb out of the slough, and only she
　Could give him so much cause to stay alive.

A blank, the day he fell on Fuji-san,
On his return to consciousness and thought,
　And every day he languished in Japan
　The only constants that he ever sought,
　On which he would increasingly depend,
Were she and all the letters she would send.

III

What had Scarce Begun

Far better off without him she would be
And what she saw was left of him was not
The him he'd ever wanted her to see.
For some time thence he couldn't speak a jot,
His voice lost somewhere in the fall. But what
To speak? Nine thousand feet his sliding fall,
He didn't really need to say a lot:
That fall from icebound Fuji said it all.

One little painting, having passed the test,
Was shown in the Academy somewhere,
And three months long it hung with all the rest,
But neither of them saw it hanging there:
Perhaps they lasted twice as long as one,
But twice too long for what had scarce begun.

Veronica

I had no right to preach about her weight:
I too have put on weight in my old age.
Take people as you find them, don't engage
Your every thought in trying to dictate
The limits to expect in excess freight,
The mega-brain of Socrates the sage,
The speed of Usain Bolt, the power to gauge
Our own talents. They seldom are as great

As we may think; our views are often short
On objectivity and common sense,
And all our theories, feelings, tenets fraught
By others' overwhelming evidence.
Be kind, avoiding judgment of her flaws,
Lest one day she reciprocates with yours.

Sue

A postcard still he keeps from twenty-nine
Years past. To their dismay he'd not display
His care for her though hers for him would shine
Out of her eyes. But why drive her away?
Too late was he to be contrite that night
She left before the light of day. Her dawn
Would never break again, no earthbound flight
She took, and to another morning borne.

Of very few he knew had ever cared
For him, so many signs could leave no doubt.
A scapegoat she, completely unprepared,
He'd snared her, only then to cast her out,
To let one woman see, upon a whim,
The way that womankind had treated him.

15 Forebears & Warfare

Anglo-Saxon Chronicles

Alfred the Great was a shy king
Who found it not much to his liking
Making do with cornflakes
'Cos he'd burned all the cakes
While hiding his face from the Viking.

King Edward the Elder
From the moment he beheld her
Shared exactly the views
Of his twenty-stone wife Eadgifu's.

King Æthelstan's
Unacceptably murderous plans
Involved spearing Saint Cuthbert
On the point of his halbert.

King Edward the Martyr,
His claim to the throne a non-starter,
Only wanted a life without hassle
But was sadly killed at Corfe Castle.

Æthelred the Unready
Felt rather heady.
Territorial gains
From his war with the Danes
Left him moderately flushed and unsteady.

The Great Dane Sweyn Forkbeard
Would frequently walk weird.
His lumbering limp
Made him look like the wimp
The lusty old Bishop of York feared.

King Edmund Ironside
Was glorified countrywide,
And was better known for his valour
Than his thanatognomonic pallor.

King Canute entered into dispute
With his courtiers hot in pursuit.
No matter, the tide
Was to shatter their pride
And refute his omnipotent repute.

King Edward the Confessor's
Comedo expressers
Left his mirrors unreflective
And consequently ineffective.

Hereward the Wake took umbrage
At outcasts from Cambridge
But associated more freely
With exiles from Ely.

Robart Strong, Buried 1583

Some four-and-a-half centuries ago
They buried at West Kirby church this man
Whose life enabled mine to be and so
Project his being far beyond his span.
I picture him at work in netherstocks,
His leather jerkin shabby and well tanned,
A beard and shoulder-length his curly locks,
With cap and baldric, fardel in his hand.

And strange to think did he but abrogate
The great imperative to propagate
His progeny he might have spared their blight
Of ceaseless toil. They never asked for breath
To breathe on earth, each day a drawn-out death
For every crying soul that craves the night.

A Seventeenth
Century Ancestor

John Jones my forebear, blacksmith by his trade,
    Was born in Storeton, lived in Landican.
    And when he rode his grey one day he made
    His way to Woodchurch where the clergyman
    Would pray for him and all his progeny
    If they would pay their tithes and let him roar
    And rant against the wealthy tyranny
    And rail against the idle and the poor.

"When we invent the car we won't want your
Profession any more," the churchman scorned.
"When we've explained the world away and why
We die, and why your pompous sermons bore,
    I'd fly to hell myself to see you fry,
We won't want you or yourn," the blacksmith yawned.

My Grandfather

I

A Life of Austerity

My grandfather was always old. The more
I think of him the more I call to mind
He seldom left his kitchen. We would find
Him sitting in an upright chair, the door
Pine-panelled, high ceiled, lino on the floor,
And he would sit there all day long behind
A newspaper. The place for me defined
Him like the horrors of the First World War.

You see it spoke of his austerity.
He dwelled, like all the old in reverie,
A lifetime in his prime. Sometimes he went
To sleep, his nightmares we could only guess.
Sometimes again we saw an immanent
Serenity, a twilight peacefulness.

II

Trotters and Tripe

A man of simple needs he was and so
Indeed was he a man of simple taste.
He lived upon a spartan diet based
Upon pigs' trotters, tripe and offal though
It did him little harm. I didn't know,
But now in retrospect, I should have placed
Him there on high among the gods. Shamefaced,
It's far too late to say I didn't know.

For nothing less than patriarch he was,
And of his wisdom we knew nothing for
We couldn't ask him anything because
To ask would show we didn't know before.
Pigs' trotters, tripe and offal he would chew
And that I think was all we ever knew.

III

A Biscuit Tin

But in a biscuit tin behind a door
Beside the hearth among old dog-eared snaps,
Of long-forgotten kith and kin perhaps,
His father on a bicycle we saw
Who died in nineteen ten, not long before
All hell broke loose. Amid the other scraps
We found inside their careless little wraps
Were all his letters home from the Great War

One hundred years ago, and all forlorn
His honourable discharge creased and torn.
Could he still hear the pounding of the guns
Resounding to a barrage from the Huns?
For if by chance upon the Somme one day
We saw it in his eyes he didn't say.

Gallipoli 1915

There are none left on earth can ever tell
At first hand of that mortal waste of war
Hard-fought one hundred years ago and more,
The stench of death, of corpses left to swell,
Their startled eyes wide open where they fell.
No mockery of sleep their faces bore
But ghastly grins, with twisted limbs they wore
Too well the look and smell of Brueghel's hell.

And all those flies! Those awful feasting flies
That crawled on every living thing and dead.
Nobody warned them of the loathsome flies!
Nobody said they bred and fed and spread
And filled the air and blotted out the sun
From all who fell beneath it one by one.

Gallipoli 2015

Today the site, serene and clean, the one
The tourists see. They chatter as they view
The endless ranks of war graves; many too
Still marvel at their youth, the lives undone,
Wiped out before the barrel of a gun.
Recruited under age some never knew
The heavy odds against survival through
The hecatomb, their living scarce begun.

I look for urchin shells at Suvla Bay,
A blameless place. One hundred years before
Were four untried battalions put ashore.
A boy among them landed here that day:
My grandfather, to fight the Turk, engage
In brutal war at sixteen years of age.

The Battle of the Somme 1916

Some nineteen thousand British soldiers died
That first day in the Battle of the Somme,
To trade a patch of mud a few yards wide.
If they survived the fighting they'd succumb
To dysentery, trench foot, diarrhoea.
Far better, for my grandfather, a burst
Of shellfire hit him just behind the ear,
And he was honourably discharged first.

The zeitgeist then meant willingly he'd gone
Straight from the flies, the horror and the stench
Of death that was Gallipoli, and on
To France to face extinction in the trench.
"So sweet and fitting," Horace sweetly said,
Not fitting him though: Horace died in bed.

The Highland Bagpipes

At Monte Cassino my father caught
Some shrapnel in his back and yet in spite
Of this he went on worthily to fight
And liberated Venice, so he thought.
The doge himself was utterly distraught
And froze with fright. The populace took flight,
They fled the Scottish regiment, their plight
The fiercest onslaught Venice never fought.

With march and reel, with pibroch and strathspey
Their victory the pipers would convey,
They fondly felt that Venice would enjoy
The ghastly din. And worse it grew and worse;
The pipers thought the people cried for joy:
They mostly wept for otherwise they'd curse.

16 Doctors & Plumbers

God Bless the NHS

I must confess the NHS
Is in a pretty awful mess
Yet I'd assess it does possess
So many virtues in excess.
But nonetheless our happiness
We must assess by our progress,
And at a guess I'd say success
Eludes us in the NHS.

Too many doctors will express
Concern, too many will obsess
About our health, on H&S
And fears about the NHS.
No-smoking signs cause much distress
For smoking is not dangeress [sic].
I smoke in bed and I profess
It's hardly deleteriess [sic].

In theatre they should all confess
Incompetence, cackhandedness
Afflict them. They should tell us, "Yes,
What we don't know we have to guess."
The freedom of the British press
Does mean that we will have to stress
We may be seeking full redress
In missives to the NHS.

Fred's fifty fags a day far fewer: (less,
My uncle waives grammatical finesse)
Don't count the ones he smokes in women's dress,
The ones that clearly gave him more distress.
For double pneumonectomy the name
Bilat'ral orchidectomy's the same.
Confusing these of course is no-one's fault,
No need for post-operative assault.

So here we have a massive compo claim.
Of course it's not about the money, NO!!!
But no-one else must go completely lame
As he has, questions must be asked. We know
How to address the issue and engage
Stakeholders round the table. Now we need
Collaborative access at each stage,
Transparency and buzz-words guaranteed.

We need to let the country know that half
The patients hogging every packed-out ward
Have Munchhausen's syndrome. They 'ave a larf
At us: free bed and board is their reward.
God bless the overburdened NHS:
The stress they're under vital to success.
At least one operation went so well
Without the squeaky voice you'd never tell.

Overstretching the NHS

(And the Sonnet)

When patient queues lose patience and abuse
Our omnisapient doctors' views it's time
We locked their proctoscopes away. Sublime
Per rectum are the telescopes we'd use
The fattest we could find: we'd all enthuse.
Who needs trephine or microtome when crime
And NHS infractions climb? Let's chime
In with the nation's notions and amuse
Ourselves with sundry louts' ablations. Who's
To get the NHS back in its prime,
Redivivus from this primordial slime?
Let's win the peace and every ward effuse.*

Abominable chiropractors know
Abdominal retractors often blow
A fuse electrocuting some to show
Just what a painless way it is to go,
To stifle forthwith our sigmoid and
cyclostomous chasms,
To freeze all our sneezes and diaphragmatical spasms.

*or "war defuse."

The Nursing Profession

Halfway across the Brooklyn Bridge I see,
Recalled from sixteen years ago, the way
A woman smiled at me, a nurse, a ray
Of light, she blazoned her humanity.
Ten years before, down snow and ice and scree
I fled the summit of Mont Blanc, a prey
To labrynthitis in a storm that day.
One storm I left, the other followed me

To London where I retched with every sway.
But no-one flinched, and why I cannot say.
At Chelsea and Westminster where they dealt
With me a pat upon the back I felt:
A trainee nurse, spontaneous, unversed,
Her outburst of compassion unrehearsed.

Bad Workmen and their Tools

They say bad workmen always blame their tools,
A platitude and not a valid claim.
More true it is to say offensive lame
Remarks bring shame on he who ridicules
Our artisans and plumbers for the fools
He thinks they are. Good workmen work the same
As bad with pointless awl and nails, and aim
For average with broken plastic rules,

Cracked socket wrench and pliers, brace and bit,
Blunt craft knife, augers, nothing that will fit,
With toothless padsaw, jack-plane, threadless screws,
Blunt chisels being all they have to use.
Good workmen blame their tools as by default:
While backing such Pavlovian assault.

Before Major Surgery

Sometimes some die under the surgeon's knife,
Released from all their cares upon this earth.
A painless way to quit this futile life,
For some of us a torment since our birth.
How many of us would go through it all
Again, had we the option not to be?
We never asked to linger here to fall
At every hurdle, at the end to see

Our shattered hopes, our efforts come to nought,
To leave no trace but footprints in the sand.
And our release is very dearly bought
If we must needs await His dire command.
What power the surgeon wields could spare the strife
That cumbers ours to end this mortal life.

The Botanist

No flowers in his book can emulate
Our summer verdure, here in lifeless state.
Like shrivelled parchment, bloodless veins embrowned,
No longer nurtured in the fertile ground,

No longer bowed nor steadfast in the gales,
Nor reaching for the open sky, mares' tails
Above, no rich and fruitful earth below,
The scent of roses can no longer blow.

Pressed flowers, relics. Little else remains
Upon this yellowed page where once the rains
Bejewelled slender stalks with diamonds bright
And speckled leaves with loveliness and light.

And no more will they ever meet the dawn,
No more their stems can bend to greet the morn,
No more their leaves can rustle in the breeze
Nor wind can sough among the willow trees.

And once the flower is plucked, its nature gone,
What virtue can there be preserving one
That cannot move, no longer interplay
With light and shade, can only fade away?

The contents of this book we see, the same
On every page and labelled with the name
Of each in copperplate about it writ,
With Latin words wherever it will fit.

And all these blooms once taken from the ground,
Their vibrant colours withered all around.
Magenta, crocus-yellow, cobalt blue
All now a drab ecru or biscuit hue.

And every flower identical we see,
Each specimen, its immortality
Assured inside the covers of this book
Where none but dismal bores will ever look.

17 Bogmen
& the
Afterlife

Apocalypse

I

How will I find you in the fire and ice,
In the great nightfall of total eclipse?
Beyond the dark somewhere lies Paradise,
Beyond the splintered wreckage of our ships
Of war, Dreadnoughts, Polaris submarines,
The might of armies and the might of man!
Our nuclear missiles, all our war machines
Were known to Him before the world began.

Compare ours with the devastation wrought
By acts of God. The Pantocrator brought
Ten plagues to Egypt and old Noah's flood.
And trumping Scripture's vision our resort
Today: could fission shed as much lifeblood
As intergalactic collision would?

Apocalypse

II

How will you hear me now above the sound
Of trumpet blast and crash of stormy sea?
I need to make amends for being me,
For every grievous fault regrets profound
When things I said and didn't say compound
The pain I gave to you. And I agree
There have been times like others I foresee
Become more precious every day I've found.

The memories turn nightmare from despair.
If I but knew you were still here somewhere
Then I would mount Olympus Mons and I
Would plumb the depths of the abyss and cry
"Please tell me how and where I will find you:
Or was your passing bell our last adieu?"

Apocalypse

III

How will I know you or will you know me?
When every bird has hurtled to the ground,
And every whale and every fish has drowned,
And every beast, engaged in killing spree,
Has eaten every one that cannot flee;
When all our merchant ships have run aground
Whose crews, surviving tidal wave, have found
On land no respite any more than we

Can find remission in abyssal deeps,
Aloft among the Himalayan steeps,
Long buried in the pure Antarctic snows
Or stranded on remoter polar floes.
Into its scorching core may I be hurled
If so I cannot find you in this world.

Apocalypse

IV

Where will you be at the last trumpet call,
At Armageddon's final martial blast?
From Babel, Ur and Jericho each vast
And monumental last great city wall
Will fail, the unassailable will fall,
Our ship will sink no matter how steadfast
The helmsman, all his years before the mast,
Should hurricane force twelve or worse befall.

Then siren-like the sounds should we count down,
Submerged, how long it takes to choke and drown,
Then strand on foreign sand reborn as we
Upon some lorn sequestered isle and be
The mistress she as I the master of
The raging seas and raging skies above?

Apocalypse

V

When will I find you at the end of time?
Among our ancient forebears in their graves
With cavemen, longbow men and galley slaves,
And men-at-arms deep in primordial slime.
Those fletchers primitive, the sweeps who climb
Our chimneys, ploughmen, publicans and knaves;
The bowyer strings his bows, the paviour paves
The pavements and the poet pens the rhyme.

And so much talent, skills long-since forgot
Lie mouldering still in peat and claggy soil,
In tons of earth in every garden plot
The produce of our tireless sons of toil.
And bound below each mound deep underground
Profoundly sleeping, talents lie unfound.

Our Trials on this Earth

Why do we sorrow so much here on earth?
Why do we undergo such needless pain?
To fill the sadist with his evil mirth,
Perhaps, we suffer otherwise in vain.
We need to feel the pain to let us know
When something's wrong with us, to put it right.
But animals, they cannot tell us so:
Their torment seems no more than deadly spite.

He sends us avalanche and drought, fire, mud
Slide, earthquake, storm and catastrophic flood
To indiscriminately kill the good
And innocent among us. And so should
We heap upon Him holy hymns of praise,
In hopes to fathom His perplexing ways.

The Afterlife

Has anybody kept a rendezvous
With one in Paradise or long since hurled
Into the deep abyss, or wading through
The cold grey tundra of some netherworld?
"The bourne from which no traveller returns"
Might be the hell of Bosch or Brueghel, may
Be Rodin's Gates but nobody confirms
The truth of it, no-one will ever say.

And someone told me once "It's all pretence;
It cannot be," said he, "We've all been conned.
An afterlife defies all common sense."
Dismissive, he, not easy to respond.
Beliefs instilled in us we hold till death:
They rarely change from birth to dying breath.

A Vision of Hell

It's so much better that we never know
The time, the minute or the hour, the day
Those gaunt grey fingers grip our hands; the way
The psychopomp will lead us down below.
No charnel house, still bleeding corpses show
All round them blight, corruption and decay,
Bones flayed of flesh their foetid reeks convey,
The haunt of stabbing rook and strutting crow.

But one still quick among the dead will be
While through the grating of his ribs we'll see
This beating heart still beating. Let him weep:
Who sow the wind, the whirlwind shall they reap.
No creeping wretch is this, his pain long done,
For it is I, my torment scarce begun

Grauballe Man

He lies exposed to view in this glass case
Exactly as he lay three hundred years
Before our Christ was born, between his ears
Torn open with a savage force: his face,
All blackened by the peat who in disgrace
Perhaps or battle died, betrays his fears.
Behind those narrow eyelid slits he peers
Uncomprehendingly to outer space.

That hollow void bore his intelligence,
Inside those sockets now no evidence
Of who he was or how it was, the way
He died that day; and we can only pray,
Express dismay and say how glad are we
To be and not to be as dead as he.

Lindow Man

Upon an undernourished constitution
His punishment so very very harsh,
A cruel and protracted execution
Its finer details best left in the marsh.
We back away from closer meditation:
Pete Marsh we call him, for it helps to lend
Us distance, such a comic appellation,
So long ago he died it can't offend.

I wonder sometimes does a breath of life
Still fan that peat-discoloured brow sometimes
Across the moss when stabbing like a knife
The cold north wind descends from icy climes?
Our reverential awe he'd gladly waive
For peace and quiet and a lonely grave.

Tollund Man

Poor Tollund Man was buried and the rope
They hanged him with, deep in a Danish bog.
We don't know why it was he had no hope
But hanged he was, they hanged him like a dog.
But someone tenderly would keep the peat
Out of his eyes and close his mouth to save
His tongue, no woollen shawl nor winding sheet,
No mortcloth in his dismal sodden grave.

Unwilling witness he, perhaps, to such
Barbaric cruelty and far too much
To bear, or was it guilt that made him screen
Those sightless eyes from things they might have
seen?
And was his hanging fair, and was it right?
Or was he murdered in the dead of night?

A Ditch-Dog

I wish that I had never seen its eyes.
They loom out of the mist from years ago,
Mauritian beauty everywhere, I know,
Faint wisps of cirrus, powder-blue the skies.
Skin-deep and from afar its charm belies
A closer look, what horrors dwell below.
A culvert blocked by this great dog and so
Just left to rot or dumped here for the flies.

The stagnant waters couldn't flow although
The rains may fall and storms may come and go.
Eyes open, opaline, a ghastly white,
In tresses pondweed partly hid the sight
And there with glassy vacant gaze it lies:
If only I had never seen its eyes.

18 Holy Men
&
A Black Sheep

Gerard Manley Hopkins

Let him pity his own heart more. Resigned
Though disinclined, so bravely he'd forbear
From born proclivities, and rarely spare
His anything-but-gay tormented mind.
A tortured intellect and wont to find
That love and lust went hand in hand; unfair
It is they are so near aligned: despair
He fought, at war inside with half mankind.

Though images forbidden come and go
In constant flow yet oh! did he but know
Far better ones his errant thoughts condemned,
From self-restraint much finer feeling stemmed:
And with his fire-folk he found treasures of
The mind, his heaven in the stars above.

Saint John Southworth

So here he lies as he has lain in state
These ninety years in this cathedral crypt
At Westminster. We come to venerate
The relics of a martyr: his heart, ripped
From his chest at Tyburn for a priest,
Was sewn back in at Cromwell's stern behest.
Four times arrested and three times released,
That blessèd little man four times confessed.

His derring-do his daring deeds display,
This doughty representative of Christ.
Our fathers' faith, so compromised today,
A travesty for all he sacrificed.
With face behind a silver mask he lies
And if he cries we cannot see his eyes.

402

Sir Thomas More

No Doubting Thomas he, nor need he strive
To tell *why* Lutherans should burn in hell.
These heretics beyond redemption fell;
If More could not, then how could God forgive?
He chained them to the stake too late to shrive
Their hell-bent souls. And yet did Christ not tell
Us "Do as you would be done by?" How well,
Then, does it square with *roasting men alive?*

Though writing to his dearest Meg conveys
Such tender thoughts, his published works report
The earthy, ribald coarseness of his phrase.
We judge him far more gently than we ought.
And while our years may see our faces lined
Five hundred more for More seem more than kind.

A Silver Sixpence of 1581

Though now a church and convent here we see,
It was in penal times no hallowed ground.
Saints Edmund, Ralph and Alexander found
A gallows built for three. A quiddity
Of thought their crime to some it seemed to be,
They garnered sympathy from all around
Who heard the sounds no Smithfield could
have drowned,
Their bloody quartering at Tyburn tree.

And may this clipped and tarnished coin
Have helped vouchsafe an early end, enjoin
The bedesman beg the Lord for wings to flee?
A silent witness may this tester be
To shrieks and howls from these poor dying things
And witness to the peace the silence brings.

Saint Margaret Clitherow

A matron born in Bloody Mary's reign,
A Queen who might have saved her from her fate,
A Catholic she and full of virtuous hate,
For Protestants her righteous disdain.
Then Good Queen Bess, devout and pious, fain
To show the vile torments that would await
All Romish priests who dared defy the state,
A dreadful end and just as inhumane.

Betrayed in York for harbouring a priest,
Her eldest still in training on the feast
Of Lady Day in Reims. There in his head
He might have felt the weight that stole the breath
From her, perhaps he knew with silent dread
That this was Margaret, slowly crushed to death.

Saint Dismas
(The Good Thief)

How dismal his demise! Did Dismas find
It difficult to feel the power of prayer
While racked with pain? How did he not despair?
On his conviction crucified, consigned
To hell on earth, then to be quarantined
To grind his teeth in purgatory where
Obligatory torments will prepare
The sinful for their future peace of mind.

No place for Dismas, purgatory, for he
Bypassed the stage through his propinquity
To Christ on that auspicious day, to be
With Him in paradise hereafter free.
And so was Dismas blessed, his soul refined,
Streamlined for sainthood, first among his kind.

The Incredulity
of Saint Thomas

If only with my eyes that I might see
Nor need put finger into His right side
Nor touch His hands or feet, for surely I'd
Believe, no doubting Thomas would I be.
If only He would deign to heed my plea,
If only I might see Him I would bide
Forever in His fold, no longer hide
My face from Him nor from His grace to me.

Nor would I even need to ask, I'd know,
Had I but lived two thousand years ago
In Palestine. How blessèd were those three
Disciples knowing Him with certainty,
Who saw Him on the mountain glorified
With Moses and Elijah at His side.

19 The Butcher of Barcelona

The Butcher of Barcelona
A Picaresque Novella in Verse

I

We tramped along the Rambla one fine day,
Chalked pavement art we found along our way,
Jongleurs and buskers, mime artistes and bawds,
Where dippers pick the pockets of the frauds.

II

A stage where acteurs manqués tread the boards,
A matador can brag of his awards.
Since no poseurs like him are ever gored
It's surely time he fell upon his sword?

III

Here scallywags lalligag, gagging for fags,
Old lags' ankle tags snagging broad Oxford bags,
Where drag queens and strumpets
and crumpet are found
And blackguards and nagging old ratbags abound.

IV

The windows of a butcher's shop we found.
From meat-hooks hanging ceiling to the ground,
Great flanks of beef and shanks of pork arrayed.
With paper lace, in pride of place displayed.

V

Beneath the weight of meat his counter groaned.
His knives were bright and sharp,
his cleavers honed
For cutting scrawny bits and chicken wings.
But what a lot of creepy-crawly things!

VI

That brace of pheasant by the front-door bell
Fly-blown it was, with all-pervasive smell.
Not even the most foul-scented peasant
Ever could have smelled so damned unpleasant.

VII

Nor he, the gory apron that he wore
And all that month-old sawdust on the floor.
This rack of lamb, that Parma ham, ox hearts;
Unpalatable, vital body parts.

VIII

Sirloin and porterhouse, prime cuts of beef,
Whose erstwhile owners sadly came to grief.
A delicacy with a shock we saw,
A fancy of the human carnivore,

IX

A pair of sucking-pigs, these creatures cursed
With nought but torment from the very first
Day of their birth. And there they lay as they
Had lain in life, not old enough to play

X

But old enough to slay. Their hell on earth,
To see no daylight from unasked-for birth
The horror of an agonising death,
Released from barely two-months' drawing breath.

XI

Those sucking-pigs as pink, disturbingly,
As still-born babes, as shocking too to see.
Sans trotters, snouts and curly tails their size
And hue the same. Those almost human eyes

XII

That looked beyond us with their glassy gaze!
If only they could but perceive some maze
Of fields, of meadow-grass and fragrant smells
That knew not Eden's fall. Now darkness dwells

XIII

Behind these eyes, the darkness of the blind,
The blindness of the dead; while intertwined,
The ivy and convolvulus both vie
For pride of place against an eggshell sky.

XIV

Unlike most avès there are no such things
As flying pigs and very few that sing.
They're rarer than a badger on the wing;
Casals with missing violoncello strings;

XV

Pablo Picasso painting someone's face
With only two or three ears when there's space
For nine. (He thought their snouts were far too big
And didn't give a fig for any pig.)

XVI

Artistic pigs are few and far between,
And rarely therefore are they ever seen,
No fetching sketch or etching has a fine
Design award presented to a swine.

XVII

Few pigs assent to, most of them resent
Our purging their pig pens of excrement.
It makes us judge them to their detriment,
And that's not just because they're corpulent.

XVIII

They do not need the light of day, we say,
And better that they sicken us: that way
We need not tender piteous remark
Since they prefer to wallow in the dark.

XIX

Does it facilitate the butcher's deed?
Abhor their table manners and their greed,
Deplore the lack of hygiene in their sties,
And execrate their latent weight and size?

XX

For surely that must be the only way
That anyone could move himself to slay
These helpless piglets in his charge, betray
Such innocents with pitiless foul play?

XXI

To kill with animosity unjust,
It helps if we compound it with disgust.
To slay these harmless creatures every day
Though, some might find it easy anyway.

XXII

We tramped back up the Rambla, long delayed.
On our return each corpse that he displayed
Like meat upon a supermarket shelf
No longer had a prior life itself.

XXIII

A few had claimed the butcher worked all night
Sometimes, his curtains drawn, his blinds shut tight;
And sometimes people heard a doleful sound
As might be heard from creatures underground.

XXIV

That night a padlock broke and failed to stop
Them breaking into his old smelly shop.
Upon a shelf a waxen human head?
"A sculpture for a flowerbed," he said.

XXV

At this we felt our fears were reconciled:
Despite his work the butcher looked so mild.
Unnoticed though by any, still he smiled,
As he cut up the carcase of a child.

XXVI

And then one day he didn't open shop,
The punters hacked his shop door down chop chop,
Then at the bottom of the steps that led
Into his dingy cellar found him dead

XXVII

With half his face and both his ears chewed off.
His leg a savage fiend had tried to scoff,
Poetic justice had been served on him,
For in one hand a small child's upper limb

XXVIII

Seen hanging in his shop the day before
As "choicest leg of lamb," the butcher bore;
And in his other hand a great "pork chop."
Or so it had been labelled in the shop.

XXIX

And when they ventured down they found inside
His cellar two enormous pigs as wide
As two barn doors, who'd never seen the light
Of day. He'd fed them human parts by night,

XXX

And processed in the day their excrement
From which he siphoned off the nutrient.
And when the butcher "went" he sent
It to augment the porcine effluent.

XXXI

There never could have been a better fluid
To complement the diet of a suid,
It made them fat and seeming affluent
This concentrated porcine nutriment.

XXXII

And these two pigs were utterly immense
World record holders, meaning no offence,
And if it made them fat it made good sense
To feed them full of farrow's feculence.

XXXIII

They'd never seen the sun nor felt the rain,
(Enough to drive the very gods insane)
But what we never know we never miss,
The cordon bleu cuisine made up for this.

XXXIV

The case was sent for trial straight away.
Ten counts of murder was the charge they'd lay
Upon the late departed slaughterman
But far too late to shove him in the can.

XXXV

And thus the butcher dodged a lengthy stretch,
As did his errand boy, the lucky wretch,
Dismembered in a pie the butcher ate
With Worcester sauce in 1928.

XXXVI

And once pushed in those pigs could not get out
And so beyond all shadow of a doubt
Could not have carried out the wicked crimes
Reported of them in The Sunday Times.

XXXVII

For in absentia a lesser charge
Was laid upon them, they remained at large,
Except they could not pass the cellar door
Nor could their digs break through the concrete floor.

XXXVIII

And so their digs were knocked down all around
These two great greedy grunters on the ground
(It made town planners sigh, dead Gaudi wince.)
A palace for a high-bred Saudi prince

XXXIX

They built, a place of such great opulence
For these two paradigms of corpulence,
With views across the Med, it's said, to die
For; satin skies above where pigs can't fly;

XL

And fertile fields below where they might "go,"
Expelling fertiliser fumes to blow
Across the fence and next-doors' residence,
Dispensing thence offensive flatulence.

XLI

But this was merely to assuage their guilt,
For pigs don't need nor want a palace built
Of precious stones and filled with affluence;
Nor interested in wielding influence,

XLII

Still dwelling in their pigsties and their dung
To live among their far-flung and unsung
And yet heroic fellow-pigs, to eat and sleep
Together and have comfort when they weep.

XLIII

These porkers got off light, their crimes so slight,
With nothing to indict them with they might
Have sued the butcher, screwed his next of kin,
An action they would have been sure to win.

XLIV

They never asked to eat anthropic meat,
Refresh themselves with human flesh and eat
Prime cuts of beef they knew with disbelief
Came from a human being. Though their grief

XLV

Could scarce compete of course and yet they too
Were victims of the twisted butcher who
Had turned his dismal cellar to an oubliette
Where he could either feed them or forget

XLVI

Those porkers he kicked down into the gloom.
The steps that led into their vaulted tomb
The butcher knew, or so he would presume
That as they grew, he'd engineered their doom.

XLVII

That noble pair of porkers, innocent
Of any anthropophagous intent
And victims too of false imprisonment
Their freedom in the end was heaven-sent.

XLVIII

For they had found the porcine promised land.
Hell-bent the butcher, on the other hand,
Proved guilty of infanticide beside
A charge of multiple suidicide.

XLIX

The Catalan is not a happy man
Without a moral to a tale that can
Improve his soul, some worthy master-plan
That mustn't leave that man an also-ran.

L

Because the human race cannot abide
An also-ran, a blessing that he died,
For all his long-term plans were overthrown,
This slaughterman was acting on his own.

LI

His aim to have complete control of man,
To introduce the wildest diet plan
Whereby for want of any other food
He'd have his pigs, and not to be too crude,

LII

(And using each pig as a guinea-pig
His target was to make them just as big
As hippos, fed on human parts while young)
Progressing in the end to pure pig dung.

LIII

The butcher's plan to try to make one day
A kind of perpetuum mobile,
A self-perpetuating humanoid
And self-sufficient, wholly self-employed.

LIV

Meanwhile the pigs were let loose, moved outside,
And given total freedom, authorised
To raid the skips, and all the rubbish tips
For pickings from discarded fish and chips.

LV

They'd scour the streets for chewing gum and butts
Of fags and scoff the offal and the guts
The angler often putts far out to sea,
With beer cans, rubbish, picnickers' debris.

LVI

For this was manna to our pigs, nor need
They covet caviar to sate their greed.
These modest grunters never would demand
Of any person for their dual band

LVII

A tax deducted from their pay at source
To fortify a Pigs' Protection Force,
No horde of henchpigs, battery of coarse
Thick peasants or a regiment of horse.

LVIII

These massive pigs, these vast humungous boars
Were humble, only eating apple cores
And hips and haws and beech-mast in the wood,
For simple fare was all they understood.

LIX

But with their new-found freedom they would dare
To blitz the skips and garbage tips elsewhere,
To rob the vineyards of their premier cru
And scrump the orchards of the well-to-do.

LX

They took entire allotments in their stride,
They emptied barns of forage and beside
They looted local supermercados.
Phlegmatic were they, no desperados,

LXI

For all they wanted were the pigswill stores
And plastic toys to exercise their jaws,
The odd few tins of dogmeat from those miles
Of aisles, these piles of serried ranks and files.

LXII

And all round Barcelona you could trust
These pigs for you'd be happy to be trussed
And stitched up like a kipper with them. Pigs
Adopted back-combed pig-tailed periwigs,

LXIII

Stood in the dock and on the witness stand,
And on the bible they would put a hand
Or trotter (though they couldn't understand
The point of the imperious command):

LXIV

"Mankind not guilty of suidicide"
They lied, "For humankind could not abide
To live with us or with themselves if they
Knew what they did to us or we could say

LXV

What dreadful suffering they put us through.
In all humanity they couldn't do
The callous things they do to us to end
Our sorry lives in torment then to lend

LXVI

Us anonymity upon these shelves,
And earn complete detachment for themselves.
The horrors of the slaughterhouse they would
Eschew if they but knew or if they could.

LXVII

Far better not to know too much or you
Might pity us for all that we go through
From sorry birth until our sorry end
No consciences have you to need to mend."

LXVIII

And then the Spanish Civil War broke out,
The people left their porkers thin and stout,
They left their livestock, worries and their bills
And fled to shelters in the local hills.

LXIX

Meanwhile the homely sties of every boar
Were flattened in that vicious civil war,
So many sows in farrow left among
The squealing remnant of their orphaned young

LXX

And lying dead, they'd smother all beneath,
A prey to vulture's beak, to rodent's teeth
Or wandering the newly opened ground,
The acrid smell of burning all around.

LXXI

For now, exposed in cellars underground
Enormous pigs, ginormous swine they found
Among few creatures to survive the blitz.
The Barcelona butcher had his wits

LXXII

About him when he craftily foresaw
The carnage of the bloody civil war.
But though he'd wisely kept them underground
Now they were free they couldn't now be found.

LXXIII

They left their livestock, all their sows and boars:
They felt no guilt in this, there was no cause
To rescue those who never started wars
For they were only pigs, they gave no pause

LXXIV

For man's concern. And some of them were kicked
Down cellar steps at home and others picked
To eat with apple sauce or left to comb
The streets of Barcelona, left to roam

LXXV

The old Sagrada so Familia,
Top brass convening caucuses conciliar,
To try to halt from being blown apart
Basilicas unfinished from the start.

LXXVI

And in the streets the pigs feared for their lives
The same as everywhere that mankind thrives,
In gutters where they were no worse off than
They were before the civil war began.

20 Left
&
Over

A Cross & Tick

The Times crossword though harder than the Mail's
Is simpler than the Listener of course.
Magnificent the Thunderer it fails
Each day to foil the great Endeavour Morse.
Subtrist this cruciverbalist, his quick
Clue-solving still leaves him a crashing bore.
Recast so arctic is his actor [sic]
Off-stage the chances are he'll never Thaw.

Socratic anagrams just fill his head
So shunning new narcotics he instead
Whisks coca, and tries leaving out the E.
Over the 'phone he's like an angry flea,
Right snappy jerk we hear from one who spoke,
Does he come over thick to Irish folk?

A Gothic Po

A sumptuous ornament, heavily gilt,
Exquisitely chiselled and solidly built.
Upon this oak bedstead no flea-bitten quilt.
With tester above it, gazunder below,
In jadeite and jasper bejewelled although
That po is a godsend should you need to go.

For painting the lily so well and to gild
In purest of gold is a goal for the skilled.
But look at this elegant item. To build
On Morris's adage a practical pot
Has some claim to beauty for what it has got
Is usefulness, otherwise charm it has not.

Around it no Walter Crane valance you'll find,
But hand-rails to help maintain balance, designed
As aids for the agèd, the weak and the blind,
A guard for the bog-brush on constant alert,
Canary long dead in a cage up his skirt,
And a courteous loo-roll dispenser called Bert.

Poetry for Prince Albert

I

There was a young Prince at Balmoral
Whose ghillies all thought him amoral;
 They spent his spondulicks
 As newts at the Queen Vic's,
Too choral by then for a quarrel.

II

While running the Great Exhibition
Prince Albert had no-one's permission
 To buy Princess Alice
 A thumping great palace
Then send her to Chad on a mission.

III

He bought Queen Vic's horses one day,
A coach and six, a bay and a grey sorrel mare.
 Regina the bay,
 Imperatrix the grey,
Bombastic and pompous and twee I declare.

IV

Balmoral he turned to a stable,
A wrecking ball through every gable.
No walls meant more space
But let's cut to the chase,
A roof makes a poor dining table.

V

From his window Prince Albert
While honing his halbert
Fell out with his pal Bert,
His courtliest stalwart,
Their screams as they fell malapert.

These are Not Haiku

I am at a loss
With haiku: too short to get
Any meaning acr

Into Shinto shrines?
To go to Noh theatre
Don't follow the signs.

No ticket? It's fun
To Nippon a bullet-train
And simply shogun.

My bonsai shrinkwrap
So none of its growth falls on
Shinto or kneecap.

Iran's gay shahs can
To a man tan better than
Japan's geishas can.

The Oxford English Dictionary

How many, trawling through his web of words,
Did Murray find inpossybyll to spell?
While technospeak he didn't have to dwell
Upon how would he cater for our nerds
Today? A lek may charm the very birds
Out of the trees, some words may even sell
Sand to the Arabs. Most of them are well
Nigh useless though, I'd say at least two thirds.

Without the word "ruelle," though, who could tell
My doctor where I sprawl each day I fall
Out of my bed and bawl, or give a bell
To golfing partners, neighbours one and all.
My colleagues surely need a word to call
That gap between my big ears and the wall.

To Boldly Go Splitting Infinitives

Was Draco among authoritarian
Rigid tyrannical disciplinarians,
So loathed by latitudinarian
And slipshod slapdash lax grammarians?

Each sentence with wanton celerity,
Effected with cruel severity,
Much longer your term in the slammer would be
For twocking his phaeton than murdering me.

But Draco was fond of long sentences, quick
To kick Solon, his son and his heir in the nick,
For flicking his toenails, licking his sick,
And picking his nose with a cocktail stick.

He'd remember the function of every conjunction,
To lengthen his sentences, strengthen compunction.
So Draco, the lawgiving father of Solon
Prolonged them with constant misuse of the colon,

Nor wasted full stops on a specious injunction
To shorten his sentence. With strepent emunction
Solon's reappraisal of Draco began,
While he snivelled his way through a
stretch in the can.

In court where his law-giving notables
Loved sesquipedalian vocables
They'd vouch for his fine legislation
Couched in Attic, enshrined for the nation,

In courts of the law
His thoughts from the floor,
So fervid they must be correct
And Draco's alone to porrect.

Fast forward a few thousand years
And suddenly everything clears.
If it's dodgy to split your infinitives
Why risk your pluperfect predicatives?

And if you should split your infinitives
Exposing in public your genitives
By accident, you will never find closure,
It weakens your confidence, strains your composure.

A man with a camera may take an exposure
And make you forever a public cynosure.
Such actions could scarcely prevent sibyl
Making forecasts much more reprehensible.

To go in the gardens of Lambeth Palace
Precipitates archiepiscopal malice.
Don't rip your zip or your sundered infinitives
May incur a syntax on all of your expletives.

Don't dampen the consulate's carpets or go
On the embassy's Gobelin tapestries, though
With acquired diplomatic immunity
You may go with ecstatic impunity.

At Buckingham Palace the Queen and the Duke
At a musical soirée decided to puke
From the Gallery: oh! What a wheeze to go
On the crowned heads of Europe and lackeys below.

The Queen's royal throne room was sacrosanct
So tanked-up prospective offenders were thanked
To go in the staterooms, to pee on the floors,
To wee on the wainscots and oak-panelled doors.

But then was enacted by royal decree,
Promulgated at Southend-on-Sea,
A law that forbade all her subjects to wee
Within forty-five miles of a tree.

Black grouse on the menu (low calorie).
What whimsy to water the gallery.
From the lap of an old concert flautist they went
To bespatter the genial Countess of Kent.

They boked, as I said, on the Countess of Kent
While poking her cleavage, extolling her scent.
A fortune on Axminster carpets they spent
Wherever the worthy Lord Gropesnork went.

They barfed on a bart's tart from Stuttgart,
They puked on the dome of the Prefect of Rome,
The gentleman's gent to the Margrave of Ghent,
And they honked on the Doge of Limoges.

While Bach from the harpsichord tinkled
Its casing was finely besprinkled.
They went in the lift and they went on the stairs
And still they all managed to give themselves airs.

Provided a quorum of three in a lift
Confession is never required. A gift
For the schoolboy. They really are such little devils,
To trump in a lift works on so many levels.

My shameful addictions and constant evictions
Exceed all predictions with countless convictions.
The longer the stretches I spend in the slammer
The greater my grasp of the lawgiver's grammar.

To boldly go, get off and begone
You may need to be just as bold as Solon
Who used up his boundless accusatives
On preterite pluperfect imperatives.

And Bach from the harpsichord tinkled,
While the stars in the night sky twinkled.
Smoking skag, dope and coke, charlie, weed
On the stairs (so THAT'S where he peed!)

And during the soirée
And to his dismay,
A considerable fluke
For the miserable Duke,

He tripped on the corgis and when he got up
He found he had totally flattened a pup.
Now Porgy the Corgi's a rug by the door,
While Bess makes a slippery mess on the floor.

"Just hearken to we," said the Queen,
"It's clearly transparently seen
We royals are royals in name,
But inside we're exactly the same

As anyone else. We choke
In our billiard rooms and we boak
In our halls and our music rooms, puke
On the servants, poke fun at the Duke."

It's right to dispute his fox-hunting pursuit,
To barf on the suit of the vulpicide brute,
To shoot the old Duke; and let no-one dispute
The lethal repute of the Marquis of Bute.

But Draco would not have been too well impressed
With bare adjectival definitives.
He'd have gone to the soirée in shorts and string vest
All because he had split his infinitives.

Gavin Maxwell

This Eden that so coyly circumscribed
His waterfall will never be the same,
Too overgrown and dismal to reclaim
The marvels that his writings once described.
His gift to all, he ably transcribed
And shared his world with us, unwise to name,
Fine prose he penned that all too soon became
The annals of a fated life inscribed.

While Sandaig thrived untrodden by the hordes
That wrought the devastation he records,
The Eden he betrayed could not unsay
In words its wonder, would there were a way:
The end for Maxwell would have been the same,
His immolation on the pyre of fame.

An Exeter Landlady

A landlady living in Topsham once said
"We only take lodgers well-dressed and well-bred,
We give them a bed,
They expect to be fed.
They are not economically viable," she said.

Too old she was and too wise to entrance
Any lodgers in hopes of a torrid romance.
"Don't give them a chance or they'll lead you a dance.
While keeping your distance take cash in advance.
How else did I finance these stonking implants?"

She compiled many crosswords of dubious merit:
Each answer was "ferret." Too soon you'd infer it.
With lewd attitude she would rudely allude
To the prudes she'd imbued with her gross turpitude
While obtruding her crudely tattooed amplitude.

Her crosswording prowess gave no cause to gloat.
Six lights would fit badger and five fitted stoat,
But this was the Mail and the clues didn't matter.
As daft as a brush she was, mad as a hatter,
She had no illusions of brain-power to shatter.

Her size 58 treble G
The finest you ever did see,
From Chudleigh to Budleigh
No finer there could be,
She'd heave 'em both out for a fee.

One day she decided she'd migrate to France.
Huge library fines would occasion her stance
And the parking charge levied by
Topsham Town Hall
On a jam jar she'd totalled, still wedged in a wall
With the knick-knacks that filled an old
bric-à-brac stall.

Dressed in a fur coat she chartered a boat
To get her to Cherbourg, to keep her afloat,
To cross the Channel and hope to reach France.
But she viewed the expanse of the sea, at a glance
Saw the holes in the hull that would scarcely enhance

Her chance of advancing her plan to escape,
Held together with six feet of parcel tape.
The next boat she looked at was barely afloat,
It was not worth a groat and nor had it the vote
Of this crafty old scrote in her stoat overcoat.

Another she found had no gunnels athwart,
No bulwarks to starboard, no rollocks aport:
As large as a barge it was, yet I'll be frank,
As a prank the boat stank, for the sale of this plank
Would've banked not a franc,
little more when it sank.

Too shallow its draught it was scarcely a raft,
And with bulwark-free gunnels abaft this old craft
Would have given a deck-swabber housemaid's knee
Then tipped him quite happily into the sea,
As it pitched and it rolled and it sank merrily.

She hired a wherry that came her way,
Its under-bunk thunderbox out on display.
To dunk dunderfunk into such a gazunder
While drunk as a skunk, though a bona fide blunder,
Would've led to a plague and nobody would wonder.

But then it was "borrowed" and sank with all hands
In three fathoms of brine on the fine Goodwin Sands.
The next she attempted to hire was the last.
Its rollockless gunnels were quite unsurpassed,
Her thoughts of migration a thing of the past.

Her son was a scoundrel, her son was a knave,
At killing small animals ever so brave.
On Dartmoor and Exmoor he'd chase every fox
For this man was a walking paradox,
With views you'd consider quite heterodox.

"When all's said and done," he revealed to his wife,
"My mind is in dire philosophical strife:
If the fox were destroyed I'd be left unemployed,
Though bereft on the planet of Tod or Pink Floyd
It's Tod I'd get shot of and Floyd I'd avoid."

When the landlady went to Torbay
She followed a stalker, "I say,
Why don't you stalk ME,
I'm aggrieved, can't you see,
For I've not had a stalker all day."

A husband or two she'd got through in her days
And for all she had nothing but infinite praise,
For those allegedly walled up in her gable,
Climatic conditions there so much more stable
And safer than leaving them under the table.

The day that her wherry had sunk by the stern
Her library books would still give her concern.
Trussed up in her fustiest dusty old ferret,
"The ferret," says she, "For me has no merit,
Unless on your bust as a must-see you wear it."

With finely defined bathycolpous array
She suddenly thought of the best way to pay
What she owed on her loans,
to discharge all her debts
On her library books, to dispense with the threats
Of court action, she knew she would have no regrets.

The ferrets and fine stoat coat she wore over
Or nearly wore over her bosom moreover
Would drive her, though living in clover to charge
A handling fee that would pay to recharge,
Enhance and enlarge that décolletage.

The library files have a record that day
Of the landlady's ferrets, a note of the way
She elected to pay: she proclaimed she was broke
But discharged all she owed them by
letting them poke
Her ferrets, relieving her debts at a stroke.

The library staff seized one of those ferrets.
"You're a goldmine to any on earth who inherits
This ferret," said they, "And despite its demerits,
There's nothing on earth we think could impair its
Mystique and unique taxonomical merits."

They pored over tedious Linnaean trinomials,
And got such a buzz out of boring binomials,
They worked day and night, this unholy alliance,
Till wholesale reliance on mental appliance
Established this ferret as unknown to science!

The tip of the iceberg, she had a great box,
Brass-bound in her attic with great heavy locks.
In spirit were specimens hidden inside,
And sallow they were, soused in formaldehyde,
Tête-bêche like sardines,
with their mouths open wide.

A great auk inherited from a great aunt,
The skin of a dodo she'd mounted passant,
Revealing her chest in the attic to show
To her lodger its contents if he'd like to know
How to stuff a dead rook or a flea-bitten crow.

With grass-snakes and vipers exposed to the chine,
The spleen of a dormouse she'd pickled in brine,
And there in a corner a human womb
In a box! Another he saw in the gloom
As she followed him silently round the room.

To her lodger that day she innocently showed
In a jar on the floor a great ugly toad.
His mother had told him and now he could see
From the look of this toad that he'd have to agree
"It's nowhere remotely as ugly as me."

She'd shown him the toad in that jar on the floor.
Though grisly they all were, a sight to abhor;
A natterjack toad and replete with its warts,
Its tedious triplicate treatment reports
All speared on a plinth of pale olivine quartz.

Despite all those long years gone by yet he might
Very well still remember the day he was hight
Completely repulsive by someone he swore
Must have known all along but not told him before.
It was all that she needed to say, nothing more.

Not even her born self-restraint could have taught
Her the value of peace, the damage she wrought
In the mind of an immature youth and a child
By words that she spoke to him, hateful and wild,
With such talk was never a schoolboy reviled!

No Abram-man nor Walsingham,
Nor assassin like John Bellingham;
No Adam's sin so long ago,
And yet it felt to him as though
No evil ever crept so low.

She'd told him quite clearly, "Repulsive you are,
Repulsive and hideously, utterly bizarre.
So steer clear of women, too loathsome by far,
Sublimation forever your ill-fated star,
You're damned like a puddock preserved in a jar."

Like the views of most callow youths he believed
Every word that he heard, every nuance deceived,
From words spoke in anger home truths were revealed.
Over time all that truth in her words was annealed
And congealed in a rift that might never be healed.

Did she worship the Lord and the Ancient of Days,
And model her ways on the God she obeys?
For nobody else did she ever need words
To harm or alarm but to charm all the birds,
All she wanted to do was to charm all the birds.

For she said that mankind far more
kindness should give,
And it's certain that's how she attempted to live,
And only in him did it seem she desired
A butt for gratuitous insult inspired,
The target for shafts that her loathing required.

How long does it take till an atmosphere clears?
Resentment though silent can simmer for years.
Though time may heal wounds and you'll
hopefully find
That peace for the body is peace of a kind,
Much rarer combined with peace of the mind.

There's far more to live for, the more we remit,
And much more to go for the more we acquit.
Reach out from the deep to the peak
though it's steep,
The more that we sow here the more shall we reap.
So too shall we laugh more the less that we weep.

But words spoke in anger cannot be retracted.
They fester and smoulder through kindness
protracted.
If all of our reprobate acts are subtracted
From all the best deeds we have ever enacted
Let's hope in our guilt we have overreacted.

Had she at long length his forgiveness earned,
Though she'd lost him so many for whom
he'd once yearned?
Did she ever retract what she spoke on that day
To him, cancel those hideous words or unsay
Them? No, not at all, that was never her way.

And if you had listened that one night in June
You'd have heard someone playing
"Au Clair de la Lune,"
On a mouth-organ, midst the flotsam and jetsam
That prettily circles the shore-line at Topsham
Exposing the newly-drowned corpse of a lamb.

The reeds of his mouth-organ played the tune
Till another joined in by the light of the moon.
That ferrety frontage could only be she
That bounced as her footwork fought tidal debris
To sing at the end of that ramshackle quay.

From here so long ago he once swam
And thought he might end like that innocent lamb.
To France he would swim,
he would drown on the way,
To the music of Bach he had listened all day,
So near to the heavens yet so far away.

The sacred music of Bach he would play
At the site that he chose on that dolorous day,
Transported to heaven, as near could he tell
By cembalo, strings, and the sounds he knew well.
How closer his soul though, much closer to hell.

And was it her ghost that he saw by the shore,
Three ferrets, that stoat ulster coat that she wore?
He gazed on that musteline bust and he saw
One woman at least, who would never abhor
Him, one woman at least and perhaps
there were more.

The type of womanhood, long dead and gone,
A mother to somebody else's son.
Her age alone meant that he could be brave,
With no need to fear her scorn she would save
Him from bleak despair and an early grave.

And she would recall him, with pity you'd find
That lodger to whom womankind was unkind
And for whom he forwent any friendships to go
Nearly breaking his neck on the boulders below
The high tors of Dartmoor's eroded plateau.

His fate to avoid them, so where would he go?
No women he saw climb the cliffs of Kernow
And far fewer yet and then so long ago
Did he see climb the tors on the moors and why so?
For their presence would better the status quo.

Their beauty he sought to avoid but how so?
From the tors on the moors to the cliffs of Glencoe
A new charm he found to embrace, and a cause.
He would climb every weekend the tors. And no flaws
Would he find in the beauty he sought on the moors.

And does she still leave her false teeth on the stairs?
Her collection of thimbles and Steiff teddy bears?
Some forty years later he walked past the home
She shared with him once and
whence he would roam
Hay Tor to the Vixen, the coombs he would comb.

His real mother never foresaw the effect
Of her words, she could never have meant to subject
Him to all of the sadness of loveless life,
All the pains and the strife with no hope of a wife
With a lonely existence that cut like a knife.

He remembered that landlady long dead and dust,
Those ferrets draped over expansive bust.
And if she returned he no longer yearned
For those he had loved who had carelessly spurned
His affections, with ghosts no longer concerned.

And forty years after she uttered the words
His mother was guilty no more than the birds.
How could she be blamed for the sake of a phrase,
For disasters he'd wrought through
his own witless ways?
How could she be blamed for the rest of her days?

And peace of the mind on this earth for the living
Is there for the taking and for the forgiving,
Worth far more than health in flesh and bone,
Or when we are dead an impressive headstone,
Is peace of the mind which is ours alone.

The Fate of Damiens

Were I to meet my Maker should I feign
Forgetfulness or beg Him to condone
The wicked sins that I have long outgrown
Since childhood's days? Could anyone attain
Celestial heights with acts so inhumane,
Without a lifelong penance to atone?
Torn limb from limb as sundered flesh and bone,
The fate of Damiens, a man insane.

Condemned from birth was he to live to be
Amusement with his drawn-out dying breath.
The executioner, how well could he
Retain the life, deny the dying death?
How long could he prolong those helpless cries,
Who in his childhood pulled the legs off flies?

The General Belgrano

Three hundred never even said farewell
That afternoon, May, nineteen eighty-two,
When General Belgrano rode the swell,
The freezing cold Atlantic blusters blew
The louring clouds, gun-metal grey above
Foul seas whipped into fury; albatross
Dashed hard against a sky that neither dove
Of peace nor warhead ever came across.

Eternal silence cannot tell the dreams
That died with them unlived; no dreadful screams
Could ever say just how it feels with lungs
When full they are to bursting, never tongues
Can speak, nor answer from the slimy deep,
Where all is shadow, gloom and troubled sleep.

The Outhouse in the Woods

It stood neglected, lonely and aloof,
Its door fast shut, engulfed in ivy, leaved
With bindweed round its pent and guttered roof.
Their trunks grew wild, whose creeping progress
wreathed
Its boarded windows, hid from all outside
What lay within. Its louring walls would frown,
It seemed. The sturdy padlocked door defied
Attempts, half-heartedly, to knock it down.

But then they took an axe one night, they flung
It wide and stepped inside. The walls had wept,
And from a hook above his body hung.
A beetle from one eyeless socket crept,
His hands and feet with silken cord were tied
And only he and I know how he died.

Einstein

I wandered lonely as a cloud,
A mushroom cloud of toxic gas.
I wish I'd died with all that crowd.
Equating energy to mass
I multiplied it by the square
Of the velocity of light.
If you had warned me: please beware!
I might have saved us from our plight.

If I'd not set the world alight
If only I might have foreseen
What I had done and put it right.
A plumber I wish I had been.
That summer's end, 1905,
I wish I'd never been alive.

Leo Zoutewelle
1935 – 2021

A Fellow Poet

Beyond his words a man I wish I knew
But never met. His gentleness placed him,
For me, among the Christly few who brim
With love, as Cuthbert and St Francis do.
And what of lesser creatures that so few
Care to recall or give away some slim
Space in our thoughts for them? As they grow dim
Their mortal souls too will withdraw from view.

And then when out of sight is out of mind
We'll find they were remembered with their kind,
By One for whom no sparrow falls and One
Whose toil goes on, whose work is never done.
In him we find achievements in his art
Acknowledge His, who sets them both apart.

Andrew Gerard Hartley
1955 – 2021

My Brother

Before the silver cord is loosed, The gold
Bowl broken and the pitcher fractured at
The well, the wheel is shattered at the vat.
The preacher will our vanities unfold,
The vanities of life as told of old. *
But then our souls return to our God that
We fear, love and obey, though where we sat
To chat we didn't speak of Him but told

Of vanities upon that final day
We met on earth. Would we in parting pay
Those eyes a second glance, our thoughts downcast,
Did we but know that sight would be our last?
Concede his body, lead his soul to Christ
Who for the whole wide world was sacrificed.

*Ecclesiastes 12:6-8

9/11

In flaming skies the smoking billows rise
That mark the ultimate depravity
Of these who shared in our humanity,
Whose motive and whose evil cause defies
All reason, twisted as the steel that lies
Exposed in shattered concrete. Here we see
The horrors fill bin Laden's eyes with glee!
Those rusting rods still prod the acrid skies

That held suspended paddling his feet
This man, his image etched on every brain,
Freed from the furnace, stepping out to greet
A cooling breeze to quench his burning pain,
A thousand feet to meet the street below
In age-long seconds twenty years ago.

A Dilemma

She told me sadly, after she had died,
He meant to masquerade as me to cheat
Me of the gift she left me while he tried
To make me victim of his vile deceit.

"I hoped," I thought, "I'd see in him as he
Grew older my enduring link, to see
Him grow whom she had brought into the world
As chrysalis or growing leaf unfurled.

To ask him to be my executor,
Chief beneficiary, inheritor
Of my estate and all my little wealth
Not thinking he would try to take by stealth

What I might well have left in my estate
(For which he may not have had long to wait)
Or did he think that I would be so kind
To let him steal from me, I wouldn't mind?

And only by remotest chance did I
Discover what he'd done to me to try
To rob me of his mother's parting gift
To punish me, perhaps, in vengeance swift

For some slight on his mother's part or mine
Remembered with thoughts vicious and malign,
Or was it just a sense of equity
That let him think that only he could be

The righteous and rightful legatee
Of all and everything, that none but he
As far as he could see could ever be,
That nobody had any right but he.

He must have known, he must have been without
The slightest faintest shadow of a doubt.
He'd realise that nothing would accrue
To him by my demise, he surely knew.

For this was nothing but attempted fraud
From one whose conscience was so deeply flawed
He cared not for his mother's kind intent
If he in any way could circumvent

Her wishes and by any means prevent
My ever laying hold of what she meant
To give me through her generosity
And bounteous impetuosity.

Presented with the evidence did he
Own up, express regret or give to me
A single shred of counter-evidence,
A solitary word in self-defence?

Should I be grateful he did not deny
Attempted theft, be glad he didn't try
To twist the facts with brazen eye contact
Or claim some specious reason for his act?

But neither of us is the winner here,
That he should live and work so very near
And I, infirm, can never henceforth ask
For any help with that four-handed task

Or any more communicate with one
Whose trust I can no longer bank upon,
And he for me as dead as she but she
Is dear to me and he could never be.

Did I do right or wrong to disconnect
All contact henceforth, in effect neglect
Her progeny though she so very good
To me and he his mother's flesh and blood?

It was a relatively small bequest.
Ten times as much her children are possessed
Of from her will. Why did he try to take
The sum that she had left me for my sake,

The sum that she with all her best intent
Had wanted me to have to represent
Her love for me, the laughter and the tears
That we had shared in more than fifteen years?

I told her once I didn't want to be
The heir to anything but memory,
For she was kind to me far more than I
Deserved, so often I would wonder why.

So kind was she to me, I wonder why
One who could no more cheat like him than fly,
Gave birth to such offspring. Am I so glad
As bad as he she never knew she had.

If only I could ask her what to do,
So scrupulously honest through and through.
I cannot ask her now she's dead and gone
So tell me what on earth would you have done?"

School Discipline

A smack upon the legs for every scrap
Of litter found in jacket pockets or
Found hidden at the back of your desk drawer.
Hair yanked around the ears, perhaps a slap
Across the face. Not wearing his school cap,
One errant boy was kicked across the floor,
Along a corridor and through the door
Into a store and beaten with a strap

Along the way. Its contents known though locked,
Well stocked this walk-in cupboard, entrance blocked
With gags and blindfolds, bloodstains on the wall,
He'd whip that bawling boy and make him crawl.
A copy of "Justine" upon the shelf,
Without his prey he'd flagellate himself.

The A-Bomb Dome in Hiroshima

The epicentre of the blast was here,
This dome, its empty ribcage, gaunt and bare,
It stands mute testimony to the day
A Superfortress, the Enola Gay,

Took to the cirrus-marbled August skies
Above Hiroshima, unwished-for prize,
Its mission: razing of necessity
By nuclear fission an entire city.

Hiroshima rebuilt itself although
The marks of trauma long ago still show.
The Dome aside, the tell-tale signs remain,
The oldest even now won't let the strain

Subside from careworn faces, cannot let
The vibrant world dismiss them or forget.
A wizened woman bent down to the ground,
She picked up in her fingers what she found,

An opalescent shard of broken glass.
She held it to the light, and made to pass
It to us while she uttered not a word.
And had we spoken she would not have heard,

Her mind elsewhere. Her friend then took her hand,
Led her away from us and we would stand
There motionless, our eyes would follow them,
As weary as all those the years condemn.

They shuffled off, bent double as they went,
A railing for support, they both lament
Events of three score years and ten ago.
Forever fixed in minds, the afterglow

Of unexampled horror won't be shed
Till every last one still alive is dead.
And yet how can we tell when that will be,
The living dead still walk among the free.

Their thoughts are not and never will be rid
Of memories of scorching flesh amid
The twisted girders and the molten glass,
The flowing tarmac and the noxious gas,

Of people torn to ribbons in the air,
The raining skies, the white blast and the glare.
And then the blackness: nothing could compare
With this except in galaxies elsewhere.

That piece of broken glass: we had observed
Such fragments in the Peace Museum, preserved
In vials with their provenance, we read,
Removed from living beings and the dead,

From human skulls, from lungs and pancreas,
From livers slivers, splintered flakes of glass,
Extracted decades later from the bones
Of patients who complained of kidney stones.

Hibakusha, those still alive, old men,
Small children then who'd never play again,
And seventy years after the event
So many living then will still lament.

There was no other means it seems, to end
The war, and this the only way to send
A message to the whole world loud and clear
That nineteen forty-five was not a year

To celebrate VJ Day but to pray
Such desperate remedies have had their day,
That sabre-rattling need no more call
For acts of nuclear warfare but the fall

Of all dictatorships, the steady rise
Of stable government, for the demise
Of rogue states everywhere they flourish and
Prosperity for all in every land.

The Rowan Tree

So long ago it was, so long ago,
The sturdy mountain ash, the rowan tree,
Stood by the house a stone's throw from the sea,
Where only marram and the rushes grow.
The haunt of raven and of hooded crow,
They'd pick among the littoral debris,
The sea-worn lumber and the shells would be
All round the house and on the shore below.

To ward its inmates from adversity
It's said, you should not cut the rowan tree,
Or chop it down, and do not shed its blood.
No good will ever come to those who would
Dispatch the ancient, gnarled and leafless tree,
The guardian of this house beside the sea.

Ring of Bright Water

The guardian of the house, the rowan tree,
So long ago it was, none could foresee
The part it played,
The household it betrayed,
And what that tree would do to him and me.

Long, long ago so many of us fell
For Sandaig and its strange uncanny spell.
When twenty years had passed,
The tree at last
Was dead, and now there's nothing left to tell

Of its existence here. One awful night,
Possessed with eldritch powers and second sight,
Upon the tree she
Cursed him bitterly,
She cursed the house and him with all her might.

She laid her hands upon the tree and burst
Forth loudly with a dreadful oath. Her thirst
For vengeance quelled,
She thought her powers expelled,
She knew that she had done her very worst.

She laid her hands upon the rowan tree,
The house is gone, so too are he and she.
She cursed him bitterly,
Long dead is he,
So too the rowan tree has ceased to be.

The rowan tree that guarded Sandaig dead,
And all that ever lived and bred and fed,
And all that worked and died
And loved and cried
And slept and wept and breathed in this homestead.

Long gone, so too the magic of this place,
And of its genius loci not a trace
And where his desk
Stood, scarcely statuesque,
A rough-hewn boulder marks the empty space.

And here a schoolhouse stands close by the site
Once filled with children's laughter and delight,
So long ago.
They didn't even know
How harsh was their existence and their plight.

For odious comparisons were few,
No other worlds they'd seen nor pastures new,
Had not a clue
That they might come into
A life beyond their narrow field of view.

And then the last remaining crofters went
And left the site deserted, to lament
Their way of life now gone,
Could not go on,
An idyll they had lost by joint assent.

Their life was hardship blessed with purity,
No more to labour, living by the sea
Or off the land,
Nor could they understand
Despite their plight how happy they could be.

Each year the hardy rowan tree revived,
Despite the winds and blizzards yet contrived
To flourish on a dearth
Of meagre earth,
It made a living from the land and thrived.

Despite the barren stony ground, it strived
With no proximity to man, deprived
Of laughter, schoolboy chatter,
Grown-ups' natter.
Still it lived, and still alone survived

A silence, bar the sea mews, deeper than
It was in space before the world began,
And rarely mild,
So cold it was and wild
And then in nineteen fifty came a man

Who changed the landscape and forever fought
To live a life no money could have bought.
His isolation won,
It bravely shone
For him in prospect, so he fondly thought.

The simple life he craved but would eschew.
A shame it was: the more that he'd pursue
A life of fame,
The harder it became
As problems and their repercussions grew.

He brought wild animals to live with him
And thought his otters happy as they'd swim
Beside him, could not see
That they would be
Far better free than captive at a whim.

And unawares, he did so much to change
The house, and all around he'd rearrange
The landscape too,
Reshape the land he knew,
To something rank, unnatural and strange.

And what had been an idyll very soon
Became a rubbish tip, a site bestrewn
With wreckage of
A mockery of love,
A marriage shorter than their honeymoon.

And she outlived him by some thirty years,
Some thirty years' regret and bitter tears,
For when she cursed
She thought she'd done her worst,
And nothing had she left of him but fears,

That she alone had brought about the end
Of every joy of his that might transcend
Misfortune, every fall,
And last of all
The death of her incorporeal friend.

An otter he had left with her, a beast
That he had brought back from the Middle-East,
Entrusted in her charge,
To roam at large,
Through irresponsibility deceased.

And she could not forgive herself for she
Had let Mijbil, his precious otter, free.
That day a roadman's spade
Was to put paid
To otter's life. And evermore was she

Despondent scapegoat for catastrophe.
And at its core the blameless rowan tree
Clung to the earth, lived on,
But now it's gone,
So long ago and so have he and she.

A dreadful fire in nineteen sixty-eight
Was to destroy the house, annihilate
The life he knew
Who could no more pursue
The idyll than could ever abrogate

The deadly curse upon the rowan tree.
No sooner had it shed its leaves than he
Was dead, forever free
From all that he
Believed that she had blighted him to be.

But long before that curse had run its course
And while its fearsome power was still in force
I too was victim, should I
Tell you why?
Both still alive then, she full of remorse?

The rowan tree still flourished where it grew
As we climbed down the hillside for the view.
My brother, he and I
We would defy
The curse, a load of bunk and ballyhoo.

The wrong track to the house we took, I led
And steeply between little cliffs we'd tread.
That wicked spell
Still worked too well, I fell,
Three bones I broke, great gashes to my head.

My brother, seeking help from higher ground,
Two Forestry Commission workers found.
They haled me to the road
Bowed with their load,
Unconscious was I then, their fears profound.

And thence by Land Rover I was to be
Transported to the local doctor. He
Would fix my broken bones,
Endure my moans
En route to Inverness Infirmary.

And while I was in hospital so too
Was he with me although I never knew,
And there to die
Of cancer whereas I
Would soon pull through as he could never do.

And that was over fifty years ago
He suffered for his art and blow by blow
It brought him to his knees
By slow degrees.
But for his legacy he would bestow

His love for animals on us despite
His contradictions: he would still delight
In shooting game
While yet he would proclaim
His deep misgivings for their sorry plight.

A fact he found it hard to reconcile,
This zoöphile, that while he could beguile
All animals and weep
With sorrows deep
The tears he shed were sometimes crocodile.

The basking shark he claimed could feel no pain
Because it had, he said, a tiny brain.
It meant that he could kill
The shark at will
It justified his slaughterous campaign.

And over fifty years ago he died.
The curse upon the rowan tree beside
The house has long expired,
No more required,
The magic tree that for so long defied

The elements is dead as he, the tree
He knew has gone at last, its spirit free,
Though he was cursed,
The tree had done its worst
And no more harm could do to him or me.

The rowan tree long dead but down the years
Its mighty force for evil it appears
Could not be quelled,
Its grievous powers dispelled,
Nor would it ease our warrantable fears.

All hocus-pocus, for this evil curse
Was self-fulfilling prophesy at worst.
No evil charm
Had done him any harm,
The idyll ended when the bubble burst.

Jim

This place as good as any to thank those
Whose kindnesses leave me eternal debts
I can't repay, whose selflessness begets
A lifelong gratitude. Their goodness flows
Like quicksilver to mitigate our woes,
Make bearable each burden that besets
Our waking hours, to banish all regrets,
To bring us peace of mind and quiet repose.

And what they have in common is the need
To help their fellow man with noble deed
And mundane chore whose motive makes immense
As marathons on seven continents
Unpacking tins on supermarket shelves:
How blest are we as they to know themselves.

No More to Say

I have no more to say, nor words to write,
But all to strive for, all my dues to pay,
And His commands must no more disobey
In sinful cause to win, nor wars to fight.
For all that I am left with is the night
And Judgment Day and trust that if I pray
To Him then I may surely find the way
She went the day He led her to His light.

She's gone, and though it seems
there's nothing worth
My longer dwelling on this barren earth,
Yet linger still I will and long that we
May meet again. If only we might be
As one once more as two of us once were
Would I endure this life to be with her.

Ingram Content Group UK Ltd.
Milton Keynes UK
UKHW012222190523
422059UK00014B/173/J